battle of
NORMANDY

Operations
Totalize and *Tractable*

Ludovic FORTIN

Drawings by Nicolas GOHIN — Maps by Antonin COLLET

Translated from the French by Alan Mckay

Histoire & Collections

Operations *Totalize – Tractable:*
The road to Falaise

At the beginning of August 1944, after a long period of almost complete stagnation, the situation of the Allied forces in Normandy was at last encouraging: although it was a failure, operation *Goodwood* to the east of Caen had forced the German High Command to thin its lines out in the west enabling the US 1st Army to break through the front in the south of the Manche Department during operation *Cobra* which had started on 25 July. The 3rd US Army exploited this success quickly by rushing through towards Brittany and Mayenne.

Above.
Shortly after the beginning of Totalize, a Crab from the 22nd Westminster Dragoons (79th Arm. Div.) crosses the "Winston" bridge at Vaucelles. The assault forces assembled in a zone which had been damaged a lot by earlier air raids and which the Royal Engineers had had to clear as well as they could.
(Imperial War Museum B8778)

REGARDING THE BRITISH 2ND ARMY, it launched operation *Bluecoat* on 30 July from Caumont-l'Eventé towards Vire and Vassy so as to enlarge the American breakthrough and protect their western flank. With operation *Lüttich* launched during the night of the 6 and 7 August, the Germans reacted violently; but despite a few initial successes, this armoured attack was finally pushed back with the help of the Tactical Air Force. The immediate outcome was to thin out the German front to the south of Caen; this was a zone where the British and the Canadians had

been moving forward with great difficulty since the landings. Hitler was doing his utmost, ordering attack after attack against Avranches in the forlorn hope of cutting the Americans off from their bases in the Cotentin Peninsula and acting on his orders, most of the Panzer-Divisionen still available moved west even though the German front was already being turned; this meant that the Germans were gradually increasing their chances of being surrounded and this was becoming more and more likely every day. The Germans were on the decline; for several weeks now they had been on the defensive and were no longer in a state to carry out such offensives, let alone exploit them successfully.

FALAISE: THE KEY TOWN
OF THE NORMANDY CAMPAIGN

In this situation, the town of Falaise became of the utmost importance for the Germans: it was an essential railway and road centre for their supply lines; it was also the centre of an area which was getting smaller and smaller through which they could hope to escape the Normandy inferno. For the Allies Falaise, like Argentan, was one of the primary objectives for the forces coming down from the north and up from the south in order to catch the German armies in Normandy in a trap; even the idea of a "great encirclement" on the Seine was beginning to seem very attractive to Montgomery, and to Bradley, too.

On the other hand the positions the Germans still held to the south of Caen were their major asset: during operations *Spring* and *Goodwood* the Anglo-Canadians had only progressed very slightly against these in-depth, staggered defences made up of fortified villages reinforced by numerous anti-tank and anti-aircraft guns, supported by an armoured SS reserve which was readily available. The open farming countryside was almost flat, with no cover for any attackers; for a long time the British had considered it as ideal "tank country" for their advance; in reality it turned out to be ideal "anti-tank country" where the Germans came out on top... Dominated by Hill 122 which was in the hands of the Germans, the terrain favoured defence and sloped upwards gently towards Falaise (the altitude increases from 150 feet and the starting point to 410 feet at Cintheaux 6 miles away). They almost regretted the bocage – the closed-in farmland! Although the Germans had been weakened on

Below.
On 6 August, some Churchill AVREs from the 79th Arm. Div. pass through the ruined outskirts of Caen on their way to their assembly zone. According to the AoS 1234 (Arm of Service) sign visible on the right mudguard, they belonged to the 6th Assault Rgt. A whole column of Shermans is camouflaged under netting along the road on the right.
(IWM B8774)

the ground and totally dominated in the air, they were nonetheless able to maintain their forces concentrated on a narrow front to the south of Caen in static positions there which were almost intact.

The failure, or the semi-success, of the operations started on the eastern flank since the landings raised serious doubts within the American High Command, but also in Allied public opinion, as to Montgomery's real strategic competence. As the head of Allied

Above.
Officers and tank crews of the 4th Can. Arm. Brig. HQ Squadron have gathered at Vaucelles on 7 August for a briefing. Judging from the sandbags surrounding the rolling gear and the earth piled up in front of the Sherman in the foreground, the men have dug their shelters under the tanks. The enemy artillery must be threatening because some of the men are also wearing their helmets, even while resting.
(H. Aikman, National Archives of Canada PA-131364)

land forces in Normandy and under pressure from Churchill, he had to silence his detractors. A week after the end of *Goodwood*, he decided upon an attack in the direction of Falaise and chose a man whom he trusted and who had already shown his mettle, Lieutenant-General Simonds, commanding the 2nd Canadian Corps. At 41, Guy Granville Simonds was one of the youngest and most talented Canadian generals; he had successfully commanded two divisions in Italy before coming to England. Montgomery instructed Simonds to be ready on 30 July for a new full-scale offensive in the forthcoming ten days. The predicament that the 21st Army Group was in regarding under-strength infantry, particularly among the British units, designated the Canadians as the most likely candidates for the new attack: they had recently been

reinforced with the 4th Canadian Armoured Division under Lieutenant-General Kitching and the 1st Polish Armoured Division under General Maczek which had recently arrived in Normandy.

OPERATION *TOTALIZE*: BOLDNESS AND INNOVATION

The new operation – the plans were ready as early as 1 August – was quickly given the name *Totalize*: like *Epsom* and *Goodwood*, it was taken from the racecourse jargon and calls to mind the "totalizor", the person who tots up the bets. Would this new operation enable the advantages gained by the previous assaults to be exploited? In order to make up for the failure of "Spring" a few days earlier and in spite of the lack of time before the attack was launched (the divisionary staffs were only warned on 2 August, and the regiments on the 4th!), Simonds very quickly put together an ambitious and innovative plan which was to enable him to break through the solid German defences; these were set up in depth and made up of two formidable Panzer-Divisionen (the I.SS and 12.SS) and three infantry divisions reinforced by artillery, anti-tank guns (particularly the Flak 88s which could also be used against land targets) and Nebelwerfers. In order to get

Above.
From left to right Sergeants Stevenson of Kirkintilloch, Dixon of Dumfermline and Keay from Perth, three Scottish NCOs from the Black Watch (154th Inf. Brig., 51st Highland Division) who are going to take part in operation Totalize. The thistle cut out from "42nd Government" tartan that can be seen on the sleeve of the battledress, and the red plume on the Tam O'Shanter, are characteristic of this regiment.
(IWM B8801)

through these two lines, Simonds planned two assault waves with an intermediate pause so as to allow the heavy aircraft time to come over again, disengage the terrain and neutralise the defences which the Germans had hurriedly moved up; this would prevent the attackers from getting too exhausted before they were able to make the most of the advantages gained, as had been the case too often beforehand. Several innovations used during *Tractable* made it a model which is still studied in Canadian military academies:

1. The attack was to take place at night and, in order to counter the enemy defence, mixed infantry and armour columns would advance along a very narrow front. The choice of a night attack meant keeping the important element of surprise, since the enemy already knew where, but not when, the Anglo-Canadians were going to attack. In spite of the obvious inconveniences, the dark would hinder German observers and spoil their aim.

2. The assault would be preceded by air raids carried out by British then American heavy bombers (in spite

Opposite page.
Near Caen on 7 August, four soldiers from the 1st Pol. Arm. Div. pose for the photographer on the turret of a Panther destroyed in an earlier fight. The Poles were particularly impatient to take part in the offensive because they were itching to avenge their defeat in 1939.
(M. Dean, NAC PA-115490)

THE KANGAROO

A few weeks after D-Day, the British and Canadian motorised artillery units started to receive the Sexton self-propelled 25-pounders on a Ram chassis, replacing the American Sherman-based 105-mm M7s used up till then. These Shermans were then going to be returned to the Americans and it was on learning of this equipment change while he was thinking out Totalize that Simonds suggested to the Americans, who accepted, that the M7s be kept on for another use...It seems that Simonds had been thinking for a long time about the possibility of transporting infantry in armoured vehicles which were better protected than the usual Carriers. Acting under his orders a group of four officers and 250 mechanics from 12 different units (mainly from the Royal Canadian Electrical and Mechanical Engineers) started to convert the 72 Priests of the 3rd Can. Inf. Div., by removing most of the ammunition racks, removing the main armament (the .50 machine gun was retained) and sealing the opening left on the glacis with armour plating, some of which had been recovered from destroyed materiel. When there was a shortage of armour plate, it was replaced by two 2.5-mm metal plates a couple of inches apart, with sand filling the gap between them. By working night and day, the mechanics managed to convert 55 machines for the first trials on 5 August and all the vehicles were ready a few hours before the beginning of Totalize. This armoured vehicle was called the Kangaroo, no doubt because this Australian marsupial carries its young in its ventral pouch. The troops quickly nicknamed it the "unfrocked priest". Theoretically it had a two-man crew and there was room for 10 infantrymen, but in fact as many as 20 were carried at times.

Although the "unfrocked priest" was supposed to transport ten infantrymen as well its crew of two, it could in fact carry more: at least 13 passengers are visible here in the compartment of this Kangaroo. The light armour of the armoured vehicle protected its occupants from light arms fire and shell bursts.
(Tank Museum 2292/E6)

of Air Chief Marshall "Bomber" Harris' reluctance!) very close to the line of attack: the first would attack by night as was their custom and the others would prepare the advance for the second wave the following day. Apart from the tactical bombers, Simonds would have fighter-bombers and medium bombers at his disposal from 83rd Group RAF and the US 9th Air Force.

3. Despite the lack of night-vision aids, in order to guide the assault columns several different guidance

devices, some of which had to be got ready and set up for the occasion, were to be used simultaneously. The 40-mm Bofors guns would fire tracer shells along the line of the attack over the advancing troops. Luminous beacons, green on the right and orange on the left, were to be attached to the end of poles planted in the ground at regular intervals and would light up the path to be followed at the beginning of the assault.

4. Moreover, Monty's famous artificial Moonlight would be used for the first time: anti-aircraft lights would be aimed skywards to light up the terrain by reflecting the beams off the clouds.

5. A radio guidance system for the leading tanks would also be rapidly created following a very simple idea: the radio transmitted a continuous series of dots and dashes and the radio receiver operator

Above.
The traffic coming from Caen was very heavy on the Nationale 158 after Operation Tractable because reinforcements and supplies had to be brought up to the troops who were about to attack Falaise. CMP (Canadian Military pattern) trucks from the 2nd Canadian Corps (cf. the insignia on the rear right of the nearest vehicle) pass the wreck - probably booby-trapped by the Germans – of a TD M10 Achilles, also Canadian.
(Tank Museum 3000/B4)

would only hear one or the other if he strayed off on either side of the line of the advance.

6. Finally Simons invented the Kangaroo, a troop transporter designed using a disarmed M7 Priest self-propelled gun; without waiting for backing from his superiors he ordered these machines to be converted starting on 31 July. So that as many troops as possible could travel protected by armour, and at the same pace as the tanks, a number of other armoured vehicles (US Scout Cars, Half-Tracks, Carriers, etc.) were requisitioned from among other Canadian units (the Engineers, Artillery, Reconnaissance, etc.).

SIZEABLE MEANS

For his attack Simonds had three infantry divisions, two armoured divisions, two armoured brigades and specialist tanks from the 79th Armoured Division (Crabs from the 22nd Dragoons, and Lothians and Border Horse Yeomanry, AVREs from the 79th, 81st and 87th Assault Squadrons, Royal Engineers, and Crocodiles from the 141st RAC), as well as a battery of AA searchlights. Almost all the artillery of the 2nd Canadian Corps and neighbouring units, i.e. 720 guns (with 650 rounds each on average), were to support the 85 000 men engaged in the operation. More than 80 000 tonnes of ammunition and supplies needed for this huge force had to be brought up to the front in two days! Simonds had faith in his men but had doubts about some of his divisional and brigade commanders: it was too late to make the necessary changes but some of the events to come proved him right. During the briefing held on 5 August at Lieutenant-General

Above.
The Canadian departure line was the theatre of desperate fighting during July. An infantryman is examining a Panther Ausf.G destroyed at Saint-André-sur-Orne no doubt belonging to the Hitlerjugend. Other Panthers from the same division, under the command of SS-Obersturmbannführer Wünsche, confronted the Canadian Shermans during the second phase of the offensive.
(K. Bell, NAC PA-130333)

11

Columns formation
TOTALIZE

Group from the 1st Northamptonshire Yeomanry and the 1st Black Watch
(Crabs from 22nd Dragoons, AVREs from the 80th Assault Squadron Royal Engineers)
at the beginning of Operation Totalize.
A column, 4 armoured-vehicles across and about 50 yards wide and 800 yards long.
Armoured vehicles 10 yards apart across the width
and every 15 yards along the length of the column.

Gapping Force

2 × Troop A Squadron
(8 Shermans)

2 × Troop of mine-clearing tanks
(8 Crabs)

1 × Troop of Engineer Tanks (4 AVREs)

Assault Force

2 × Troop A Squadron
(8 Shermans)

3 × Group of transport vehicles for armoured troops
(12 Kangaroos)

Group of miscellaneous armoured vehicles carrying the rest of the infantry battalion
(Half-tracks, White Scout Cars, Carriers, etc.)

2 × Troop of Tank Destroyers from the 6th Canadian Anti-Tank Rgt
(8 M10s)

1 × Troop of Engineer Tanks (4 AVREs)

1 × Platoon of machine guns from the Toronto Scottish Rgt (4 Carriers)

« Fortress » force

4 × Troop and Squadron HQ of B Squadron, Fort Garry Horse
(19 Shermans et 11 Stuarts)

And so on inserted into the ranks, B Squadron bringing up the rear.

Group from A Squadron, Sherbrooke Fusiliers Rgt and from Royal Regiment of Canada
(Crabs from Lothians and Border Horse Rgt, AVREs from the 79th Assault Squadron Royal Engineers)
at the beginning of Operation Totalize.
A column, four vehicles-across and about 20 yards wide, over a length of about 800 yards.
Armoured vehicles 4 feet apart and every 3 yards, in three forces, 110 yards apart.

1 × Troop A Squadron (4 Shermans)

1 × Troop C Squadron (4 Shermans)

1 × Troop of mine-clearing tanks (4 Crabs)

3 × Troop A Squadron
(12 Shermans)

1 × Troop A squadron (4 Shermans)

A Squadron HQ (3 Shermans, 1 Scout Car)

2 × Troop A Squadron
(8 Shermans)

3 × Troop of mine-clearing tanks
(12 Crabs)

1st Northamptonshire Yeomanry Regimental HQ
(4 Shermans, 8 Stuarts, 4 Scout Cars)

3 × Troop C Squadron et C Squadron HQ
(15 Shermans, 1 Scout Car)

1 × Group of transport vehicles for armoured troops (4 Kangaroos)

1 × Troop of Engineer Tanks (4 AVREs)

1 × Group of transport vehicles for armoured troops (4 Kangaroos)

1 × Group of 8 miscellaneous armoured vehicles
(Half-tracks du Medical Corps, Bulldozer,
Carriers for mortars or for towing anti-tank canon)

1 × Group of transport vehicles for armoured troops (4 Kangaroos)

Other miscellaneous armoured vehicles brought up the rear :
Carriers, Half-tracks of the Medical Corps.

Above.
A half-track, probably Polish, going by the characteristic way the man leaning on the front is wearing his beret, is crossing the battlefield littered with wrecked German vehicles to the northeast of Falaise. There are SdKfz 250s and 251s and a Ford truck, a vision which gives a good idea of the vehicle graveyards found after the Battle of Normandy.
(Tank Museum 2985/B1)

Crerar's 1st Canadian Army HQ which had been activated, Crerar reminded his men of 8th August 1918. On that day the Canadian army made the Prussians suffer their worst day of all WWI and he intended making 8th August 1944 even blacker for the Germans. He gave the general outline of the plan but on the following day, intelligence showed that the 1.S-Pz.Div. had been withdrawn from the front and was thought to be reinforcing the second line of defence so the plan was modified. In stead of being used one after the other, the two armoured divisions were to attack together during the 2nd Phase on 8 August and reach the north of Falaise on the following day, leaving the town to be captured by the infantry divisions.

TIME MUST HAVE A STOP…

Simonds' bold plan was nonetheless risky because of the time factor. There was not enough time for the units to train properly and get used to the Kangaroo. Armour and infantry were not really used to working together and even less during night fighting. Direction

and communication problems had to be taken into account; there were not enough armoured vehicles to carry all the infantry and some of the men would have to go forward on foot. The artillery would not be able to do its job properly because it would be advancing quickly and only half the guns would be supporting the attack, the other half would be following the assault force to get closer to its targets. Finally, the 3rd Can. Inf. Div. had been fighting in the front line ever since landing on 6 June 1944 and was now in need of a rest; it would only be used to support the breakthrough. This was done on both sides of the N 158 which linked Caen to Falaise; to the west, the 2nd Can. Inf. Div. under Major-General Foulkes, supported by the 2nd Can. Arm. Brig. under Brigadier Wymann, with Caillouet, Gaumesnil and Hill 122 as their objectives, followed by the 6th Inf. Brig. on foot to clean out May-sur-Orne, Fontenay-le-Marmion and Rocquancourt, all bypassed by the armoured column. To the east, the 51st Highland Division under Maj.-Gen. Rennie, supported by the 33rd Arm. Brig. under Brig Scott had

to advance through Cramesnil, between Garcelles and Secqueville to reach the east of St-Aignan-du-Cramesnil. The 153rd Inf. Brig. was ordered to take Secqueville while the 152nd Inf. Brig. on foot was to clear out the positions bypassed by the armoured column at Tilly-la-Campagne and Lorguichon.

The breaches made in the front would enable the 4th Can. Arm. Div. to the west and the 1st Polish Arm. Brig. to the east, to advance during the second phase on the afternoon of 8 August, once the US 8th Air Force heavy bombers had passed over. Their respective objectives were Bretteville-le-Rabet and Cauvicourt. It was hoped that they could be exploited later but even then the infantry's job was not over: the 3rd Can. Inf. Div. had to take Bretteville-sur-Laize, the 51st Highland was ordered to take the wood to the south-east of Robert Mesnil and the 2nd Can. Inf. Div. had to hold the flank of the breakthrough in the St-André-Gaumesnil area.

The first three battalions in each division were to travel in the armoured vehicles in six distinct columns. These were structured slightly differently depending on

Above.
**Field artillery was
not very present in
the German defence
disposition in the
Totalize sector, so the
support of the Werfer
Regiment 83 with
its rocket launchers
was precious. Here
an abandoned 15-cm
Nebelwerfer 42 is still
armed with its six
rockets.**
(IWM B7783)

whether they were Canadian or British. The latter were
slightly longer and narrower (see examples opposite)
but they were all made up of the same components:
tanks, armoured infantry, specialist armour from the
79th Arm. Div. They were 500 to 750 yards long and 45
to 60 yards wide for each regiment that was engaged,
with more than 300 tanks in all! The artillery was to
wait for the end of the RAF raid, at 23.45 on 7 August,
before firing its barrage over the attackers' heads:
340 guns would pound the German defences, moving
forward 200 yards every 2 minutes up to a maximum
distance of 3 miles. The rate of advance was twice as
fast as normal because the new entirely motorised

columns moved faster. The rest of the artillery was to
move up in the wake of the attack or intervene as and
when needed against selected one-off targets.

THE GERMAN DEFENCE

Facing this steamroller, the Germans lined
up well-backed up defences in fortified positions (at May-sur-Orne, Fontenay-sur-Orne,
Rocquancourt, Tilly-la-Campagne, La Hogue and
on the Verrières crest) but they were outnumbe-
red and made up of units of uneven worth. As an
armoured reserve, the I.SS-Panzer Korps under
SS-Oberstgruppenführer Sepp Dietrich had only

the 12.SS-PzDiv. Hitlerjugend (reduced to only Kampfgruppe Waldmüller) left and 21 Tigers from the schwere SS-Panzer Abteilung 101 which was supporting three infantry divisions: the 89.ID under Generalleutnant Heinrichs which had been formed only in February 1944, had only recently arrived from Norway and now held a line situated directly along the axis of the Canadian attack between May-sur-Orne (Grenadier Regiment 1056) and La Hogue (Grenadier Regiment 1055) both with two battalions in defence and one in reserve, plus a battalion of fusiliers on bicycle. Coming from the 25th recruitment class, in theory it was not made up of high quality troops but most of its officers and NCOs did however have combat experience. As it was horse- drawn and had no self-propelled anti-tank guns (it called itself the Wheelbarrow Division!), neither the Allies nor the Germans expected it offer anything more than a token resistance and the Germans therefore disposed the 4 500 men, the 39 Panzer IVs and 27 Jagdpanzers from Kampfgruppe Hitlerjugend on the Laize and in the valley of the Laison to support it, when and if necessary. As for the 271. ID to the west and the 272. ID to the east, these were not really affected by the bombing and were not engaged during the first phase of the attack. Eleven out of the 21 Tigers from s.SS-Pz.Abt. 101 as well as the 38 operational Panthers in the Hitlerjugend were detached to the Grimbosq sector and only took part later on.

German artillery was very present during this period of the campaign: apart from about 80 mortars, 120 divisional artillery pieces were reinforced with two heavy batteries, Werfer Regiment 83 and its 54 launchers, and in particular a brigade from the 3. FlaK-Korps, equipped with 65 88-mm guns set out in depth along the second line of defence. This last unit was unfortunately not under the command of the I.SS-Panzer Korps but of the Luftwaffe, which caused some problems when it came to using the

guns as anti-tank or as anti-aircraft guns. The defence was well provided for with machine guns and anti-tank guns (about a hundred) including self-propelled guns. German materiel was just as good and often better than the Allies' but ever since the beginning of the Normandy campaign there was less and less of it simply because the losses were not replaced.

The High Command was one of the weak points in the German defence: after von Runstedt was sacked and Rommel wounded, Feldmarschall von Kluge took over command of land forces in Normandy. He was a competent officer but he was unable to stand up to the Führer and this was fatal during the unsuccessful operation *Lüttich*. He had no hope of obtaining a lot of supplies or reinforcements and he could not rely on the almost non-existent Luftwaffe. In spite of all this, most of the Germans believed in victory and their training was generally excellent. The Waffen-SS had a reputation which was just as flattering as it was formidable; they knew that they had already contained a number of Allied attacks in this sector of the front and they were confident they could do so again with the next one despite their fear of enemy air power. The British and Canadians seemed to be very much less at ease; up to then they had suffered heavy losses for rather mediocre results and they were frightened of resuming the attack against the formidable German 88s and Panzers which were much better than their Shermans over the same sort of terrain where two armoured divisions had already lost almost 400 tanks during operation *Goodwood*.

A lot has been said about the youth of the Grenadiers in the Hitlerjugend (average 18). But the replacements for the other divisions (the 89.ID for example), as well as those for the Allied divisions, particularly on the Canadian side, were barely older (19), so it was very young men who fought each other during the last phase of the battle of Normandy; it was their officers, their training and their experience that made all the difference.

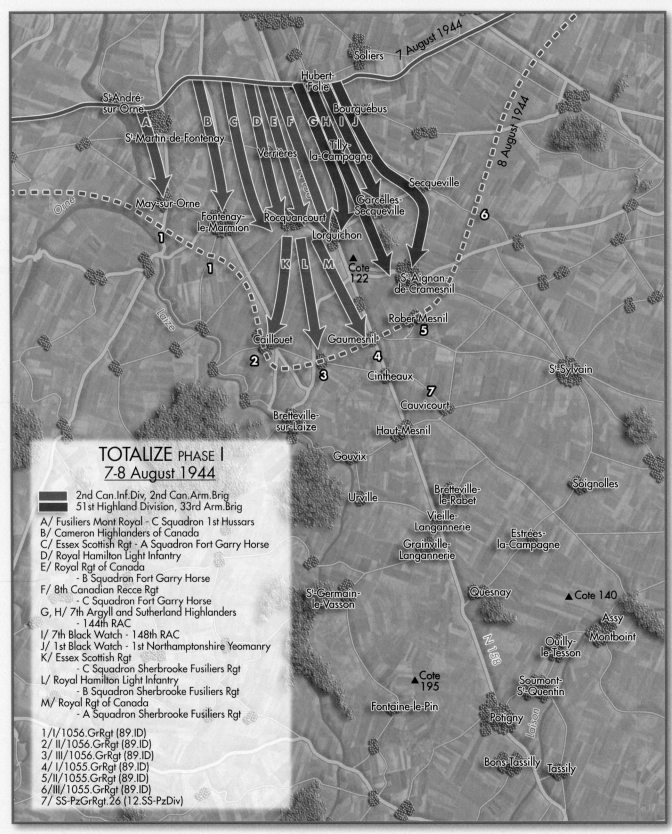

TOTALIZE PHASE I
7-8 August 1944

2nd Can.Inf.Div, 2nd Can.Arm.Brig
51st Highland Division, 33rd Arm.Brig

A/ Fusiliers Mont Royal - C Squadron 1st Hussars
B/ Cameron Highlanders of Canada
C/ Essex Scottish Rgt - A Squadron Fort Garry Horse
D/ Royal Hamilton Light Infantry
E/ Royal Rgt of Canada
    - B Squadron Fort Garry Horse
F/ 8th Canadian Recce Rgt
    - C Squadron Fort Garry Horse
G, H/ 7th Argyll and Sutherland Highlanders
    - 144th RAC
I/ 7th Black Watch - 148th RAC
J/ 1st Black Watch - 1st Northamptonshire Yeomanry
K/ Essex Scottish Rgt
    - C Squadron Sherbrooke Fusiliers Rgt
L/ Royal Hamilton Light Infantry
    - B Squadron Sherbrooke Fusiliers Rgt
M/ Royal Rgt of Canada
    - A Squadron Sherbrooke Fusiliers Rgt

1/I/1056.GrRgt (89.ID)
2/II/1056.GrRgt (89.ID)
3/III/1056.GrRgt (89.ID)
4/I/1055.GrRgt (89.ID)
5/II/1055.GrRgt (89.ID)
6/III/1055.GrRgt (89.ID)
7/ SS-PzGrRgt.26 (12.SS-PzDiv)

Map labels:
Soliers
7 August 1944
8 August 1944
Hubert-Folie
S¹-André-sur-Orne
Bourguébus
S¹-Martin-de-Fontenay
Tilly-la-Campagne
Verrières
Secqueville
Orne
May-sur-Orne
Fontenay-le-Marmion
Rocquancourt
Garcelles-Secqueville
Lorguichon
Laize
Cote 122
S¹-Aignan-de-Cramesnil
Rober Mesnil
Caillouet
Gaumesnil
Cintheaux
S¹-Sylvain
Bretteville-sur-Laize
Cauvicourt
Haut-Mesnil
Gouvix
Bretteville-le-Rabet
Soignolles
Urville
Vieille-Langannerie
Estrées-la-Campagne
Grainville-Langannerie
S¹-Germain-le-Vasson
Quesnay
Cote 140
Assy
Montboint
Ouilly-le-Tesson
N 158
Cote 195
Soumont-S¹-Quentin
Fontaine-le-Pin
Potigny
Laison
Bons-Tassily
Tassily

16

Totalize phase I: the Canadians

The eve of the attack was just as difficult for the Canadians as it was for the British: the latter had been given a ration of rum which was always a sign of hard times to come...After a hot day made dusty by all the vehicle movements, for most of the men there was no question of sleeping before the assault in the noisy, congested assembly zone.

THERE WERE STILL MANY THINGS to be sorted out like setting the navigation instruments, having another look at the plan of the attack, filling the petrol tanks, stocking up on ammunition, writing a last letter, … And all the last minute tasks that still needed to be done, e.g. for the sappers, marking out the ways through and enlarging the breaches in the railway embankments.

Operation *Totalize* began at 23.00 on 7 August with an air raid carried out by 1 020 Lancasters and Halifaxes of 84th Group RAF which dropped 3 462 tonnes of bombs on seven targets marked out by the artillery. The dust raised by the explosions was such that the last planes preferred not to drop their bombs because of the lack of visibility. AA defence was rather weak but ten bombers were nonetheless shot down. The seven armoured columns got under way afterwards across a 3 miles front. The anticipated navigation problems started almost straightaway: the compasses fixed onto the leading tanks went berserk

Above.
A few hours before the beginning of the attack, the faces of the infantrymen being transported in these Kangaroos seem to be tense. The AoS 43 sign of the 13th Field Rgt of the 3rd Can. Inf. Div. artillery is still visible on one of the tanks. It was the Priests in this division which were used for the conversion into troop transports.
(R. Barnett, NAC PA-129172)

17

because of the masses of metal all around them and the other visual aids had trouble piercing the clouds of dust and smoke caused by the air raid and made worse by the armour.

FIRST PROGRESS

Three Canadian columns comprising almost 600 tanks and formed around an infantry regiment followed parallel lines southwards: the Essex Scottish Rgt. on the right towards Caillouet, the Royal Regiment of Canada in the centre towards Hill 122 identified by green artillery markers, and the Royal Hamiltons on the right towards Gaumesnil. The advance got off to a good start at an average speed of almost 9 mph but after a quarter of an hour the leading units ran into the artillery barrage which was not advancing fast enough. Lost in the darkness, the dust and the smoke the columns started to disintegrate and scatter, while still moving forward. The specialist machines of

the 79th Arm. Div. were not spared, on the contrary. Two Flail tanks of the Lothians and Border Horse ran into each other and remained where they were with their chain-laden drums so entangled that they could not be disengaged before daylight. In complete darkness, Lieutenant Harvey, an artillery spotter from the 4th Field Rgt., working with the Royal Regiment of Canada, got lost with his Carrier. He wandered around the streets of a village until he spotted the mass of a wall on his left and ordered his driver to go more to the right. The driver told him he was already scraping a wall on the right...Harvey then held out his hand to touch the unidentified obstacle and felt the warm metal and vibrations of a tank. There was a flash of light and he saw the black cross on the German tank and managed to get away before the German tank crew, who were just as lost as he was, spotted him.

Initially on the right, the Royal Hamiltons got completely lost, crossed the path of the left hand column

Above.
Although it was taken on 6 July 1944, this shot of an RAF Handley Page Halifax four-engined bomber illustrates the atmosphere of the night air raid preceding Totalize very well. The bombs together with the luminous markers flattened the battlefield, where a lot of craters can already be seen.
(IWM C4462)

then headed off east before turning back southwards and passing by Rocquancourt on its left instead of on its right. The result was a huge traffic jam, with the two lines of advance crossing each other. They passed Rocquancourt at about 2.30 but the Royal Regiment of Canada infantry did not get down from the carriers as planned because the column leader preferred to move as far forward as possible and cross the railway embankment; with daybreak approaching, he

decided to attack Hill 122 directly with the support of the Sherwood Fusilier Rgt. which had remained to the rear. At 6.00 two companies transported by 10 Priests reached the summit of Hill 122, scattered the weak German defences and dug in to wait for the rest of the column and above all for an enemy counter-attack . This was not long in coming with German infantry and Panzers attacking along the N158 at 9.00. A Panther managed to break through the Canadian lines

Above.
This Sherman photographed on 8 August most likely belongs to the 2nd Can. Arm. Brig. since this was the only Canadian unit at the time to use track links to reinforce the armour on its tanks. The leading Sherman is a command tank, identifiable by its many radio aerials.
(K. Bell, NAC PA-114062)

Right.
A Sherman V from B Squadron, Canadian Grenadier Guards, 4th Canadian Armoured Division.

before being destroyed. The battle raged for an hour before the Germans withdrew leaving 4 Panzers and 6 armoured vehicles littering the field, but not before they had destroyed several Canadian Carriers.

THE CANUCKS MAKE CONTACT

Meanwhile at 5.30 the Royal Hamiltons got down from the armoured carriers to cross the fields towards the quarries located between Caillouet and Cintheaux.

Enemy fire halted them half way across and they had to dig in 400 yards from their objective. The Essex Scottish, which had been delayed and dispersed by the anti-tank guns to the west of Rocquancourt, reorganised before resuming its attack on Caillouet but only at 8.45. Four Panzers were spotted dug in up to the turret just in front of the village and as the CO of the anti-tank gun section did not want to use his 17-pounders and expose them to any "danger" (!),

Above. Among the 720 or so Allied artillery pieces engaged in Operation Totalize there were also some anti-aircraft guns, like this 3.7 inch British gun, which were used against ground targets in the absence of any real threat from the Luftwaffe. (IWM B9227)

Canadians and Poles assembled their long columns on the plain between Caen and Falaise, after the first phase of Totalize. Here the troop transport lorries on the left are being passed by a column of light armoured vehicles, led by a Morris Mk II Light Reconnaissance Car, which usually equipped the infantry divisions' reconnaissance regiments. (H. Aikman, NAC PA-128045)

the advance was held up until the Panzers withdrew at 14.00. With the support of tanks and artillery, the Carriers rushed ahead into the centre of the village which the infantry cleared out although the resistance was stubborn. At midday, Caillouet and its environs were under control.

Further east, 0.8 mile from the main force, a fourth column made up of the 14th Hussars and the Fort Garry Horse, also started off at 23.30; although its 200 tanks were moving up more slowly (3 mph) they too ended up running into the artillery barrage and its wall of smoke and dust. Visibility was reduced to zero with the drivers unable to see the lights of the tank in front of them. The Germans fired indiscriminately adding to the confusion. As the column advanced further away from the sources of light, the chaos became inextricable and even worsened when the Bofors guns stopped firing their tracer shells at 0.15. The advance continued nonetheless as well as it could for an hour and a half or so through the confused enemy defences, but on a level with Rocquancourt it was stopped

dead in its tracks by elements of the Hitlerjugend and some 88s; the Canadians consolidated their positions and waited for daylight.

At the rear, the 6th Can. Inf. Brig., on foot, had to clear out the German positions which had been bypassed by the armoured columns. The Mont-Royal Fusiliers attacked May-sur-Orne fighting in particular against the 1st Battalion of the Gr. Rgt. 1056. As they were too near the bombers' targets, the Canadians had to pull back before moving forward again, but towards 22.55, a German barrage dispersed them causing heavy casualties. Because of the lack of visibility, the RAF did not drop all its bombs on this target so the defence was unscathed. The Mont-Royal Fusiliers nevertheless resumed their attack at 23.55 with the support of the divisional 4.2 inch mortars. Two weakened companies led the assault, the other two were held in reserve. Heavy machine gun fire stopped the assault 350 yards from the village and artillery help was called up. Losses started to mount and even though the northern limit of the village was reached towards 2.30, the Canadians

were not strong enough to press their attack further and had to fall back. Two companies resumed the frontal attack at 3.15 while the others tried to move round on the west, but still in vain. As the road had to be secured for the armoured columns to be resupplied, Lieutenant-Colonel Gauvreau, the regimental CO, had no choice but to re-launch the attack in daytime. He was given the support of Crocodile troops from the 141st RAC, but these flame-throwing tanks needed close-up infantry protection against German Panzerfausts and Panzerschrecks and the Canadian infantrymen had not been trained for this job. Some instruction had to be improvised and this delayed the attack until midday.

PROGRESS CONTINUES

While the Mont-Royal Fusiliers were in difficulty at May, the South Saskatchewan Rgt. and the Cameron Highlanders of Canada marched against Rocquancourt and Fontenay-le-Marmion. They had no artillery support but the air raids in this zone had been more effective. They were nevertheless slowed

down by German gunfire and mines. The South Saskatchewans got hold of their objective without too much difficulty, but the Cameron Highlanders captured only half of Fontenay, suffering heavy losses from the enemy artillery; at 8.30, the Germans counter-attacked and this cut them off from their rear. Help came first from the artillery then from the two South Saskatchewan companies and then from a 1st Hussars squadron who reached them in the afternoon, once Rocqhancourt was under control. They attacked the enemy by surprise from the east. At 15.30 the Cameron Highlanders got hold of the village at the same time taking 250 prisoners. The strength of the Fontenay defence had been rather underestimated.

Above.
Infantrymen from the Toronto Scottish Regiment (the 2nd Can. Inf. Div.'s machine gun and mortar regiment identified by the AoS 64 sign) pose for the photographer in their Carrier on 8 August, near Tilly-la-Campagne. According to the little Italian flag fluttering at the front of the vehicle, at least one of these men is a veteran of the Italian campaign.
(M. Dean, NAC PA-131368)

Totalize phase I: the British

On the other side of the N158, the three British columns each comprising one battalion from the 154th Inf. Brig. (51st Highland Division), a regiment of the 33rd Arm. Brig. and the Funnies from the 79th Arm. Div., were also ready to advance. 300 yards from the road, the right hand column (7th Argyll and Sutherland Highlanders and the 144th RAC) had to capture Cramesnil and the Haut-Bosq crossroads.

Above.
The crew of the Firefly "Houghton" from C Squadron of the 1st Northamptonshire Yeomanry (33rd Arm. Brig.) is storing the ammunition racks with the heavy 17 pound shells in the radio operator's post, which was accessible only from the outside. Note the German helmet protecting the right headlight.
(IWM B8793)

THE 7TH BLACK WATCH and the 148th RAC were following the same route just behind them 45 minutes later, then turned off at an angle towards Garcelles-Secqueville to the southeast. On the left, the 1st Black Watch and 1st Northamptonshire Yeomanry column's objectives were Saint-Aignan and the orchards of Delle de la Roque. The two side columns set off at 23.30 after the aerial bombardment. Soon there was

confusion because in the darkness, the smoke and the dust, it was almost impossible to head in the right direction. The two navigation lead tanks of the 144th RAC's column fell into deep craters and Lieutenant-Colonel Jolly, the regimental CO, had took take the lead. Soon afterwards a shell fired off from the rear set fire to one of the tanks: no one ever found out who fired it... It is true that the Engineers recovered several tanks with shell impacts

7 August, the 1st Northampton Yeomanry gets ready for the night attack. The tank in the foreground is a Sherman I Hybrid, made up of the chassis of an M4 with the cast front of an M4A1. The tanks have gathered in the countryside without needing any camouflage in particular because of Allied air superiority.
(IWM B8805)

on the rear of the turret or the chassis; sometimes the Germans waited to be bypassed before opening up on the tanks, but it is also likely that some of the machines were hit by "friendly shooting"...

The left hand column crossed the railway embankment by the breach made in it at les Fresnes, then caught up with the artillery barrage at Bourguébus. The Crabs were called up in order to clear a minefield and the artillery got ahead again. The armour went past Tilly-la-Campagne and suffered losses from the defenders' heavy firing: the axis was still south/southeast but the vehicles were getting more and more scattered. At 2.40, the signal was given for the infantry to get down from the armour at some distance from St-Aignan, behind a thick protective hedge. They then they realised that the tanks could get through the gaps in the hedges, so two squadrons of Shermans went through and gave covering fire to two infantry companies up to the next hedge, 300 yards from the village. The attack started at 3.45 but the enemy defended desperately and several

Right.
An NCO from C Squadron of the 1st Northamptonshire Yeomanry distributing "Compo Pack" rations to the crews on the eve of Totalize. The turret of the Sherman I "Helmdon" in the background has been lightly camouflaged with jute strips on netting.
(IWM B8796)

25

dozen men were lost; but the enemy was forced to fall back abandoning 40 prisoners. A defensive perimeter was then set up around the village. For the loss of eleven killed and 58 missing, the line had advanced 4 miles through the German lines.

ADVANCING AMIDST CHAOS

On the right the Argyll and Sutherland Highlanders and the 144th RAC were making good progress in spite of the bomb craters and German shooting. As elsewhere, the column gradually broke up which meant it had to regroup later, about 500 yards from Crasmesnil at around 6.00 before the infantry got down from the Priests and advanced towards the village over open ground, protected by the Shermans' machine guns and canon. After brief but fierce fighting, the objective was captured at around 7.30.

At the rear, the 3rd column started at 0.15. It was made up of only 129 vehicles because the preceding column was supposed to have cleared the terrain. For almost two hours it advanced against weak resistance then headed for Garcelles-Secqueville. Leaving the

Carriers the infantry attacked at 4.30 and took an hour to capture the village. Defensive positions were then installed but the German artillery caused heavy losses.

THE TILLY GRENADIERS

While the 153rd Inf. Brig. was deploying around Bourguébus, the 152nd Inf. Brig. was moving up on foot behind the armour; the Seaforth Highlanders cleared up the terrain between the side columns from Hubert-Folie up to Tilly-la-Champagne which it then had to capture before dawn with the support of a troop of 17 pounder anti-tank guns and machine guns from the 1/7 Middlesex Rgt. Opposite them were three companies of the Gr. Rgt. 1055 (89.ID) to defend Tilly and its environs. Three companies of the 2nd Seaforth attacked Tilly from three different directions at 23.50, the artillery's moving barrage accompanied the infantry as closely as possible, and there was little resistance. But 20 minutes later enemy heavy machine guns and artillery opened up. In spite of this the infantrymen assembled for the final assault which was launched at 4.00; A Company was very quickly pinned down by a hail of bullets, B Company tried in vain to go round by the east and C Company, sent up as reinforcements for A Company also got blocked, suffering almost 50% losses! At 2.00 Lieutenant-Colonel Andrews, the regimental CO, asked for reinforcements; D Company from the Seaforth Highlanders joined the halted infantry but the situation was too confused to send further troops before dawn. An artillery battery was got ready to enable the two Seaforth battalions to carry out an attack on this all too narrow front. After another unsuccessful assault by the 5th Seaforths at 5.00, their CO, Lieutenant-Colonel Walford was ordered carry out an attack with his two battalions just before dawn. Fortunately for them the start of the operation was held up by the fog enabling them to use a squadron of 148th RAC Shermans which had become available. The tanks emerged by surprise on the south- eastern flank to pound and machine gun the enemy positions. Just before the infantry went in, the Germans asked to parley: 30 men surrendered joining 19 men taken prisoner in the area. Now at 11.00, Tilly had been reduced to rubble but was at last under control. 130 Grenadiers from the 89.ID had held out against two British battalions.

Meanwhile, to the east of the N158, the 5th Camerons marched on Lorguichon. Bottlenecks and craters considerably slowed down their progress and Brigadier Cassels (152nd Inf. Brig.) ordered them to move up closer to the road itself as early as 1.30. The advance was still very slow and the wheat, which had not yet been harvested, was more than three feet high hiding a number of snipers lying in ambush who had to be taken out one after the other. The two companies only reached Lorguichon at 3.30 which was secured 75 minutes later with a pincer movement. The British were firmly dug in defensively at 9.00.

FIRST SUCCESS

At midday, although several pockets of enemy resistance still had to be reduced there was no doubt that this first phase of the operation was a success both for the Canadians and for the British and that their tactics had paid off in spite of the bedlam: seven objectives had been reached and five were about to be; a 4 miles wide and 4 miles deep breach had been made in the German positions with relatively low casualties (only 380 men) but against stronger resistance than anticipated. This breakthrough would appear to be rather inadequate but it was in fact very large for this zone of the Normandy front. On the ground, there seemed to be no need for the second strategic bombardment because it seemed possible to exploit the situation as it was. All that was needed was to let the two divisions loose in the breach for the front to break up quickly. But this second bombardment had been obtained with great difficulty and nobody, and particularly Simonds, wanted to drop it; unfortunately the pause before the bombardment introducing the second phase gave the Germans enough time to get themselves together again.

Right.
An SS-Scharführer from the 12.SS-Panzer-Regiment of the Hitlerjugend. In Normandy the Waffen-SS camouflaged tank crew combat uniform frequently, and for the crew's own good, replaced the traditional black uniform of the Panzer crews. The "green pea" pattern was particularly effective during the Normandy Campaign and even though the crews were supposed to fight from inside their Panzers, heavy tank losses during the summer of 1944 meant that many of them fought on foot as simple infantrymen…
(Reconstruction.
© Militaria Magazine.)

The german reaction

During the first hours of operation *Totalize*, there was no doubt that the german defence was stunned and very close to being routed.

Above.
On 7 June 1944, Tiger 205 was photographed while the schwere SS-Panzer-Abteilung 101 moved up to the Normandy front. This tank was Wittmann's usual mount, but he led his final action on 8 August using Tiger 007 belonging to SS-Sturmbannführer von Westerhagen, the battalion CO.
(RR) (see text Wittmann Totalize)

ALTHOUGH IT WAS UNDER-STRENGTH (for example it only had one of its PaK 40 anti-tank companies available for use), the 89.ID, which had only moved up into the line during the night of 6-7 August, did not react so badly. But its adversary brought into play such overwhelmingly strong forces that it was not surprising the division was knocked from its positions. Its real losses were difficult to estimate but they were reasonably low initially because it was more the psychological and physical shock dealt by the Allied air and artillery bombardment that broke up the German defences. Small islands of resistance certainly managed to slow down the flow of Allied armour for a while; a few tanks were destroyed but most of the forward positions were overwhelmed. On the other hand fortified villages like Tilly-la-Campagne resisted much longer.

On the 7th in the evening, von Kluge ordered Dietrich to send the Hitlerjugend towards Condé-sur-Noireau to counter the threat of operation *Bluecoat;* the first units left during the night. Two hours later waves of bombers crushed the attack zone and it was immediately clear that a large-scale offensive was in the offing. From the very beginning, Oberführer Kurt Meyer, commanding the SS division, understood that because the 89.ID's front had been driven in, a new line of defence now would have to be positioned on the Potigny Heights and Le Laison. From his knowledge of the terrain – in 1942-43, he was the head of the reconnaissance regiment of the 12. SS-Pz.Div. billeted at the time in the region - Meyer knew that the banks of this little, closed-in river were very marshy thereby making it a good anti-tank obstacle. What he had to do was delay the Allies at all costs while waiting for the 85.ID to arrive. This was another infantry division which Dietrich had been promised and which could fill the breach.

At dawn Meyer went to Urville where the HQ of Mohncke's SS-PzGrRgt. 26 was located and, with the growing light, watched the Canadian and British armoured columns as they advanced slowly but relentlessly southwards. He then rushed to Cintheaux where one of Kampfgruppe Waldmüller's anti-tank platoons was set up. On the way he managed to regroup some troops from the 89.ID who were fleeing (at least this is what he says he did in his memoirs), then he returned to Urville which General Eberbach, the 5.Panzer-Armee's CO, had reached coming from 89.ID's HQ. They agreed they had to react rapidly and 20 Panzer IVs together with 10 Jagdpanzer IVs from the 12.SS-PzDiv. were dispatched with the s.SS-PzAbt. 101 Tigers towards St-Aignan-du-Crasmesnil, to support KG Waldmüller and the I.SS-Panzer Korps escort company. The line of the attack was drawn to the east of the N158. Artillery support was provided by the Hitlerjugend cannon and one or two batteries of the Werfer Rgt. 83 rocket launchers. The 12.SS-PzDiv.'s FlaK-Abteilung set up an anti-tank screen around Bretteville-le-Rabet and KG Wünsche and its Panthers were urgently recalled to take up positions to the northeast of Potigny.

FIRST COUNTER-ATTACK

The counter-attack was planned for 12.30 and while the units were assembling on the start line, Meyer surveyed the front next to Waldmüller from the Gaumesnil Heights . He watched the long, stationary enemy armoured columns, and could not understand why they had halted if the Germans' first line of defence had been driven in and the second line of defence was still inadequately defended. Suddenly he made out a Pathfinder launching its tracer rockets and realised that another air raid was imminent. Aware of the security margin usually respected by the Allied heavy bombers, Meyer got his troops to move up as near to the frontline as possible, thus evading most of the bombs. As the swarms of four-engined bombers filled the sky, an SS grenadier was heard to cry out: *"What an honour! Churchill has sent a bomber for every one of us."*

The second phase of operation *Totalize* had just started.

Top, right.
SS-Hauptsturmführer Michael Wittmann at the height of his success in July 1944 during the ceremony to award him the Swords to his Knight's Cross with Oak Leaves. It is almost certain that he perished, blown up by a Firefly in the 1st Northamptonshire Yeomanry.
(RR) (see text Wittmann Totalize)

2nd Canadian Armoured brigade

50 Brigade Headquarters

51 — 6th Arm. Reg. (1st Hussars Regiment)

52 — 10th Arm. Reg. (The Fort Garry Horse)

53 — 27th Arm. Reg. (The Sherbrooke Fusiliers Reg.)

Schwere SS-Panzer-Abteilung 101 / 102

 3 Cie Commandement 3 Tiger

 14 Cie de Combat 14 Tiger

 Cie Anti Aérienne

 Cie de services

 Cie de réparation

Left.
B-17 Flying Fortresses from the 390th Bombardment Group drop their bombs somewhere in Europe in 1943. Trained to hit targets in enemy territory, the American crews developed a method whereby a lead bomber gave the rest of the group the signal to drop their bombs, which was the cause of tragic mistakes during Totalize.
(IWM HU4052)

Left.
The bombs dropped in the air raid preceding the second phase of Totalize fell too close to the Allied units, as this shot shows. Soldiers probably belonging to the 3rd Can. Inf. Div. according to their Mk III helmets which they were already wearing on 6 June are sheltering in a ditch and looking with concern at the columns of smoke rising a few hundred yards away.
(NAC PA-154826)

Totalize phase II

On the morning of 8 August 1944, 681 B-17s of the US 8th Air Force approached Normandy. The Pathfinders identified their targets accurately, marking them out with coloured flares in conjunction with the red British and Canadian artillery marker shells.

ETWEEN 12.26 AND 13.55, 497 heavy bombers dropped 1 487 tonnes of bombs on the narrow front line in front of the Canadian 2nd Corps. Most of the other planes did not drop their load because of the lack of visibility but others dropped their bombs well off-target and in spite of the 1 500 yard safety margin, just as Kitching and Maczek had feared, there were some tragic accidents. For example a lead "ship" in the 351st Group was hit by flak and dropped its load by accident. As a result its entire group did the same, as was the practice in the USAAF. Everything fell on the Allied lines and a total of 65 Canadians and Poles were killed, at least 350 were wounded, a number of vehicles were destroyed or damaged. The chaos was indescribable in the ranks of both armoured divisions which had had already had a lot of trouble getting organised on their departure line because of the craters and the night's traffic jams. Morale was also low, particularly among the Poles as it was their baptism of fire.

CANADIANS AND POLES IN THE LEAD

On either side of the N158, both armoured divisions nevertheless managed to get under way at 13.55 as

Above.
The 4th Can. Arm. Div. went over to the attack in the afternoon of 8 August. Sherman Vs, probably from the Governor-General's Foot Guards, rushing in a column towards Falaise. The third tank is a Firefly, recognisable by the long barrel of its 17-pounder gun.
(K. Bell, NAC PA-140822)

planned, the Canadians on the left and the Poles on the right. Only the leading elements could advance; the others were still trying to get organised or reach the departure line. The artillery units in particular could not give any support because some of them had not been able to set up their firing positions; others were tending their wounds or trying to re-establish their lines of communication following the USAAF's "friendly bombardment". The armour advanced slowly and cautiously. Although they were new to the game, the tank crews in the two divisions knew that what they had to fear most of all were the German anti-tank guns... All the potentially dangerous positions were systematically surrounded and cleaned out, a cautious and effective method which was not exactly what Simonds had had in mind when he conceived this armoured "charge". Moving up through the 2nd Can. Inf. Div.'s and the 51st Highland Div.'s defensive positions caused bottlenecks which slowed down the advance even further. Little by little the 1st Polish Arm. Div., gaining confidence in itself, acted sometimes daringly, but the 4th Can. Arm. Div. lagged behind, to Simond's anger. When the division's CO, Lieutenant-

General Kitching, came to 4th Can. Arm. Brig.'s HQ, he found Booth, the CO, asleep in his command tank. He told him off, ordered him once again to make a quick advance, but without much success. A group comprising elements from the South Alberta Rgt. and the Argyll and Sutherland Highlanders had nonetheless made good progress and taken Cintheaux. It had even reached Le Haut-Mesnil whose northern section was taken at around 19.00; the group then found itself blocked in a neighbouring quarry by a battalion of the SS-PzGrRgt. 25 and infantry from the 89.ID which were retreating. A few 88 mm cannon brought forward by Meyer to the north of Potigny got to grips with the tanks from the South Alberta Rgt. which tried to go round them. The Canadians preferred to consolidate their positions at nightfall and withdrew their tanks from the front line.

Meanwhile to the east of the N158, the Poles advanced with more and more self-confidence, the 2nd Arm. Rgt. and the 24th Lancers pushing on to Saint-Aignan in tight formation. They suddenly ran into KG Waldmüller's anti-tank guns and Panzers

Below.
On 8 August across the open plain to the south of Caen, near Cintheaux, a Sherman from 4th Can. Arm. Div. HQ, identified by the AoS 40 sign on a black background, leading a column of Carriers southwards. Damage from air raids and the fighting is visible on the trees in the distance or on the telegraph poles in the foreground.
(K. Bell, NAC PA-131373)

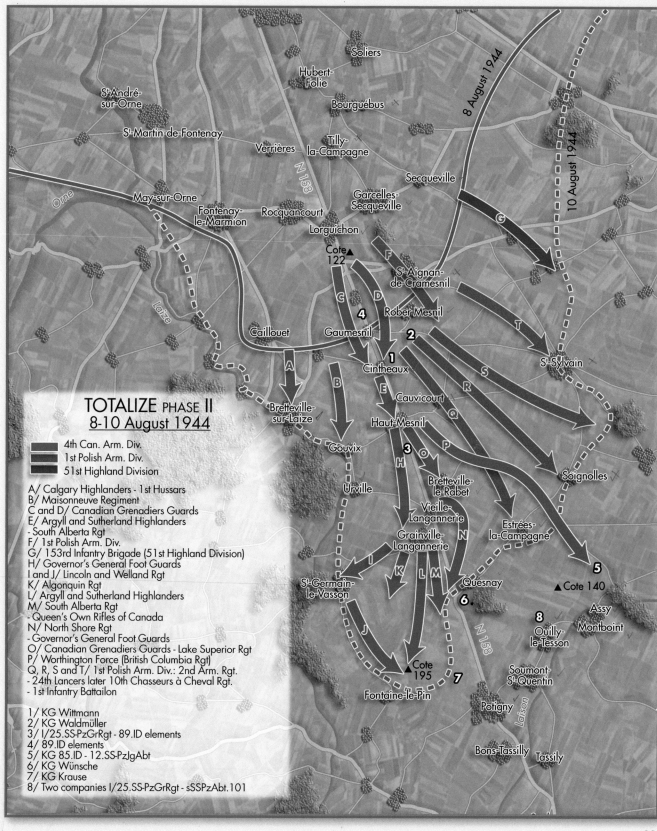

TOTALIZE PHASE II
8-10 August 1944

■ 4th Can. Arm. Div.
■ 1st Polish Arm. Div.
■ 51st Highland Division

A/ Calgary Highlanders - 1st Hussars
B/ Maisonneuve Regiment
C and D/ Canadian Grenadiers Guards
E/ Argyll and Sutherland Highlanders
- South Alberta Rgt
F/ 1st Polish Arm. Div.
G/ 153rd Infantry Brigade (51st Highland Division)
H/ Governor's General Foot Guards
I and J/ Lincoln and Welland Rgt
K/ Algonquin Rgt
L/ Argyll and Sutherland Highlanders
M/ South Alberta Rgt
- Queen's Own Rifles of Canada
N/ North Shore Rgt
- Governor's General Foot Guards
O/ Canadian Grenadiers Guards - Lake Superior Rgt
P/ Worthington Force (British Columbia Rgt)
Q, R, S and T/ 1st Polish Arm. Div.: 2nd Arm. Rgt.
- 24th Lancers later 10th Chasseurs à Cheval Rgt.
- 1st Infantry Battailon

1/ KG Wittmann
2/ KG Waldmüller
3/ I/25.SS-PzGrRgt - 89.ID elements
4/ 89.ID elements
5/ KG 85.ID - 12.SS-PzJgAbt
6/ KG Wünsche
7/ KG Krause
8/ Two companies I/25.SS-PzGrRgt - sSSPzAbt.101

33

Shermans from the 1st Pol. Arm. Div., recognisable by the insignia on the transmission block of the first tank, driving across devastated countryside to cross the Orne and reach their departure point, on the morning of 8 August.
(K. Bell, NAC PA-128954)

which had remained there after the failure of their counter-attack. Nearly 40 Polish tanks were destroyed or damaged and the attackers had to fall back in disorder towards their departure line. After spending two hours re-forming, the Poles started off again but much more cautiously this time. By evening they had barely progressed 1 mile and had not yet reached the Cintheaux-Saint-Sylvain road. At 2nd Canadian Corps HQ, Simonds was furious because although they had been supported by the heavy bombers, his two armoured divisions had only advanced 1-3 miles! At 21.00 he ordered the attack to continue during the night and therefore Booth sent the 4th Can. Arm. Brig., split into two tactical groups (Halfpenny Force and Worthington Force) to take Bretteville-le-Rabet and Hill 195 to the north of Fontaine-le-Pin respectively.

Right
Firefly Vc, 144th RTR,
33rd Armoured Brigade

The german counter-attack

A short while after the air raid which missed them almost entirely, the units assembled by Meyer went over to the attack against the Canadian and Polish armoured columns.

ELEMENTS FROM KG WALDMÜLLER, meeting south of Saint-Aignan advanced immediately under the artillery barrage and towards 12.55 reached some hedges to the north of Gaumesnil where they took a breather before continuing on towards St-Aignan. They were spotted by A Squadron, 1st Northamptonshire Yeomanry, which destroyed the leading Panzer. The others headed off to the northeast, still hugging the hedges and surprising a small British armour convoy. In the fierce skirmish which followed, the 1st Northamptonshire Yeomanry lost twenty or so tanks but the full weight of the fire from the artillery, the

anti-tank guns, the machine guns and the Shermans drove off the Germans who left 11 Panzers including 5 Tigers behind them on the battlefield.

Sturmmann Wiese was the driver of one of the Panzer IVs in the 12.SS-PzRgt's 5th Company, which took part in the KG Waldmüller counter-attack. During the Panzer charge, his tank was hit and brought to a standstill; smoke started creeping into the compartment. The tank commander ordered them to bail out but Wiese's hatch would only open a couple of inches, and the flames leapt in immediately. It was the Schürzen, the light armour plates protecting the tank from hollow

Above.
This SdKfz 251 half-track from the Hitlerjugend whose insignia is clearly visible on the frontal armour, is armed with a strange canon, an Italian light gun perhaps, obviously fed by a magazine. The SS-PzGrRgt.26's 3rd Battalion and a little reconnaissance group were the only units still using such armoured vehicles in the sector to the north of Falaise. (ECPAD)

charges and anti-tank rifles, which were in the way and Wiese had to get out through the radio operator's hatch. With the two surviving crewmen, he got out under fire from the enemy with his clothes on fire. Returning to the German lines he lost consciousness gradually without noticing that he had been wounded. In a feverish, semi-comatose haze lasting several days

and after half waking up painfully several times, he only realised on the 21 August that he had been captured by the 1st Polish Arm. Brig. when he came to in a Leeds, England hospital bed.

By rounding up three weak infantry battalions, Waldmüller had managed to attack several times but in the end at around 14.00 he had to recall his forces to

1st Polish Armoured Division

Commanding Officer :
General
Stanislaw Maczek

10th Chasseurs à cheval (reconnaissance)	Machine gun and Mortar Battalion	Tanks : 10th Armoured Brigade	Infantry : 3rd Chasseurs Brigade	Artillery	

| 1st Armoured Regiment | 2nd Armoured Regiment | 24th Lancers | 10th Dragoons (motorised) | 1st Battalion of Podhale Chasseurs | 8th Chasseur Battalion | 9th Chasseur Battalion | 1st and 2nd Motorised Artillery Regiments | 1st Anti-tank Regiment | 1st Anti-aircraft Regiment |

89. Infanterie-Division

Commandant :
General Leutnant
Conrad-Oskar Heinrichs

1055	1056	189	89	189	189	189
Grenadier Regimenten	Grenadier Regimenten	Artillerie Regiment	Füsilier Bataillon	Pionier Bataillon	Panzerjäger Abteilung	Aufklärung Abteilung

their base. The British were able to hold out thanks to a shuttle operation using Carriers and Stuarts organised to resupply them. In spite of heavy losses, Meyer was satisfied because he thought he had brought the Allied offensive to a standstill. In fact, this halt had been planned a long time in advance, as mentioned above, and although the vigorous German reaction did worry the Allies a little, it did not change their plan. The negative consequences of this counter-attack were perhaps more serious for the Germans than they imagined...

THE END OF A LEGEND

Among those taking part in the counter-attack was SS-Hauptsturmführer Michael Wittmann, the ace of the German armoured arm, who was moving northwards with four other Tigers from sSS-PzAbt. 101. Since his own tank (N°205) was being repaired, he had borrowed Tiger N°007 from the command platoon. He did not like this mount very much because this command tank carried 30 less shells than the others so as to have enough extra radio space. While the German infantry and tanks clashed violently with the attackers, Wittmann advanced along the N158 to the junction between the two Allied columns and fired at the Shermans belonging to the Canadian Grenadier Guards.

The group of Tigers then split up, with two Panzers now attacking the Poles while Wittmann carried on northwards. But when the three Tigers were on a level with Gaumesnil, they opened fire on the Sherbrooke Fusiliers on the left, exposing their right flanks to the

guns of the Northampton Yeomanry which was still holding the objectives it had reached during the first phase of *Totalize*. Lying in ambush in an orchard, N°3 Troop from A Squadron was in the ideal position. Captain Boardman, second in command of the squadron ordered his gunner and the three other 75-mm Shermans in the Troop to fire at the enemy's turrets. At that distance (about 800 yards) their shells had little chance of piercing the Tigers' side armour but they could distract the crews while the Troop's Firefly got its angle of fire right. Aboard this Firefly commanded by Sergeant Gordon, the gunner was Trooper Joe Ekins but he had only tried his 17-pounder out once during training! Gordon positioned the Firefly; Ekins got the rear Tiger in the line in his sights and fired twice. The tank caught fire. The other Panzers replied and the Firefly had to withdraw but a ricochet hit the small turret hatch and this knocked Gordon out. Lieutenant James from N°3 Troop took his place, repositioned the Firefly and ordered "fire". A single shell and Ekins blasted the turret off the second Tiger. The third Tiger was going round in circles no doubt damaged by the 75-mms; it was finished off with two rounds. It burst into flames. In only a minute a single Firefly had destroyed three Tigers! And Wittmann, the ace with 138 kills was in one of those Tigers. Balho, the radio operator in one of the other Panzers (Dollingen's) recalls seeing the side of the Wittmann's tank being pierced by a shell; several other witnesses saw the turret of a tank explode (according to a snapshot of Tiger 007, it was definitely

Previous page.
The Poles who got to England with the greatest of difficulty to take up the fight again and liberate their country were in a hurry to have a go at the Germans. The crews of these Shermans have already learnt, from the experience of their elders no doubt, that the big white identification stars on their tanks had to be hidden because they often offered all-too-beautiful targets for the enemy.
(IWM B8823)

Right.
The Tiger I belonging to Hauptsturmführer Michael Wittman during Totalize, from the schwere SS-Panzer-Abteilung 101.

Opposite page, top, right.
Another shot of the 1st Polish Armoured Division vehicles assembling. The Sherman in the foreground is a model from the earlier series, equipped with direct vision blocks for the driver and the machine gunners. In the background is a heavy Scammel Pioneer recovery tractor.
(IWM B8830)

Wittmann's mount). Ironically, the same Firefly was destroyed a few minutes later. Ekins managed to escape from it and was put in the reserve. He became a radio operator in another tank and for the rest of the war never had the opportunity to use a 17-pounder again...

The theory an eye witness expressed at the time suggesting Wittmann's tank was hit by a rocket launched from a Typhoon has been taken up by some authors but it does not stand up to close scrutiny. At that precise moment of the battle there were no Typhoons over that particular part of the battlefield and no pilot ever claimed to have destroyed a Tiger on 8 August 1944. On the other hand tanks from the Sherbrooke Fusiliers

or the 144th RAC, which were at the right range, might possibly have taken part in the end of the "Wittmann Legend".

THE WORTHINGTON GROUP'S TRAGIC FORAY

The Germans took advantage of the night of 8-9 August to realign their front, and to reorganise and resupply. Half KG Krause, formed round the SS-PzGrRgt.26's 3rd Battalion, fell back onto Hill 195. The remainder withdrew between Soumont and Ouilly-le-Tesson whilst KG Waldmüller (including the Hitlerjugend anti-tank battalion) set itself up on a line running from Hill 134 - Hill 140 - Maizières. The Panzers, including

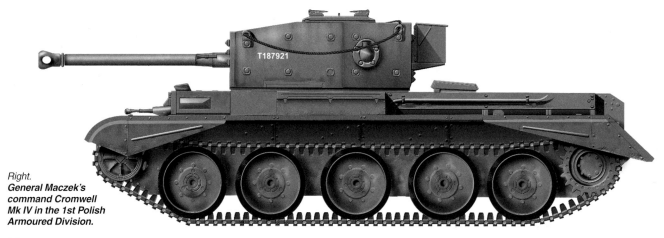

T187921

Right.
General Maczek's command Cromwell Mk IV in the 1st Polish Armoured Division.

6 Tigers, were assembled in Quesnay Wood, sheltering from the Jabos, on a position dominating the battlefield. They were joined by KG Wünsche with its 39 Panthers and its imminent reinforcements in the shape of the 85.ID and 13 sSS-PzAbt.102 Tigers. The artillery, the mortars and the Nebelwerfers also fell back, more often than not to the south of the Laison.

On the Canadian side, the British Columbia Rgt. and two companies from the Algonquin Rgt. formed the core of a force commanded by Lieutenant-Colonel Worthington which had to attack at night over 5 miles and get hold of Hill 195 to the north of Fontaine-le-Pin. At 4.00, after only four hours' preparation, Worthington's force set off from Gaumesnil led by the British Columbia Rgt.'s C Squadron. Near le Haut-Mesnil it soon ran into the Halfpenny Force column heading towards Bretteville-le-Rabet; Worthington therefore decided to turn southeast and then back northwest. But after advancing for more than one and a half hours under sporadic fire from the Germans, the column got lost and did not head northwest as planned. At 5.30, a hill came into sight. Although they did not recognise the area from their maps, Worthington and the leading elements thought that it must be Hill 195. Despite misgivings expressed by the column's other units, Worthington's force nevertheless headed for the hill which in fact was only Hill 140, situated to one side of the N158 between Estrées-la-Campagne and Soignolle, more than 4 miles from the initial objective! At 6.00 the Canadians ran up against KG Waldmüller which was falling back, knocking it about a bit and causing quite heavy losses

Above.
This column of Shermans which stretches out over the Normandy plain belongs to the 1st Polish Armoured Division, as the black initials PL on a white oval indicate, like the country stickers on private cars. The AoS 51 sign on a red background identifies the Senior Regiment of the 10th Armoured Brigade: the 1st Armoured Regiment.
(IWM B8826)

Another view of the same canon shows the damaged shield, and the gun's destroyed tractor, no doubt a French made half-track going by the tracks still visible. The I.SS-Panzer Korps had a hundred or so anti-tank guns in the 2nd Canadian Corps' zone of the attack during Totalize.
(IWM B8832)

in armour and men. At 6.55, Worthington signalled that he had taken Hill 195 and set himself up defensively to wait for reinforcements from the 4th Can. Arm. Div. Everybody on the Canadian side was convinced that this information was accurate, but the Germans had spotted that this enemy group was in fact behind their lines and got ready to counter-attack at once.

Worthington's force comprising 55 tanks, a company and a half of infantry and a few anti-tank guns assembled on Hill 140. The rest of the column had got lost and never joined the rest of the group. SS-Obersturmführer Meizel, who had run into Worthington's force when he had tried to join KG Waldmüller which itself had engaged the Canadians, reported what he knew to Wünsche who responded immediately by sending the Grenadiers from KG Krause with 15 or 18 Panthers (two companies on bicycle from the 85.ID joined the group later). Meyer had also seen what was happening and he ordered KG Waldmüller to counter-attack with the support of 5 to 8 Tigers. Two assault groups therefore converged on Hill 140 from Quesnay Wood, the first from the front, the second by going round by the south-east. Fighting started at around 8.00 with the Panzers easily destroying 12 Shermans from a long way off, taking advantage of their cannon's

A Cromwell from the reconnaissance regiment of the 1st Polish Armoured Division passes in front an 88-mm PaK 43/41 destroyed during the attack; it was a formidable adversary whose shells easily pierced the armour of all the Allied tanks. Note the camouflage on the shield and the 88-mm barrel.
(Tank Museum 1800/E5)

greater range. Worthington immediately asked for support from the tactical air force and artillery, which he obtained quickly... on Hill 195 - since the coordinates were erroneous. The SS tightened their grip and Allied communications were broken off towards 9.07. The 4th Can. Arm. Div. hurried the Governor General's Foot Guards' tanks to the rescue of Worthington's force, but in the wrong direction...Hill 195.

On Hill 140 the fighting was fierce; Worthington ordered the seriously wounded and the prisoners back to the rear on the available half-tracks. The column managed to get through the tightening German noose but in the general confusion nobody managed to explain exactly what situation Worthington's force was really in. Moreover, Typhoons attacked the Canadians on Hill 140 thinking they were Germans. The planes only stopped

Previous page, top.
After the fighting, Wehrmacht prisoners are escorted to the rear by men from the 51st Highland Division. The NCOs in the centre and on the right, recognisable by the white edge to their collar, are wearing a campaign insignia, a shield, that of the Crimea or the Kuban, on their left sleeve. They are therefore veterans and not new recruits.
(IWM B8818)

When Totalize was re-launched on 9 August, the troops advance had to be re-organised in order to avoid bottlenecks and congestion. Lance-Corporal Armstrong gives information to Lance-Corporal McDonald on the Bretteville-sur-Laize road, at a control post of the 51st Highland Division (cf the initials HD on the signpost).
(M. Dean, NAC PA-160831)

On 9 August Troopers Gaudet and Scott of the South Alberta Rgt. examine a signpost showing the way to Langannerie, Urville and above all, Falaise. Although it was only a few miles away, the birthplace of William the Conqueror was not to be captured until ten days later...
(H. Aikman, NAC PA-132413)

strafing when they saw the yellow signals sent up by Worthington's force and in the end turned upon the "real" Germans. Once again the lack of communication between aircraft and land forces meant that the information about this mistake was not transmitted either.

At the beginning of the afternoon there were only 8 operational tanks left on Hill 140 and Worthington decided to try and breakthrough to the north. The tanks managed to reach the Polish lines and the truth about the mistake finally came to light but it was too late. Each from their own side, the Poles and the Grenadier Guards tried to come to the rescue of the Worthington force, but they were brought to an abrupt halt by the heavy barrage coming from Quesnay Wood and the approaches to Hill 140. At 18.30, the SS launched a terrible assault against Hill 140. Any Canadian who could bear arms took part in the defence with grenades and light weapons. Worthington was killed in the fighting and shortly afterwards the survivors saw the Poles coming to their rescue being driven back. At dusk, several successive German attacks ended up by overwhelming the Canadians and only two groups of seven men managed to get out and rejoin the Poles. In all 120 survivors managed to get themselves off Hill 140 which had held out for 14 hours thanks to everybody's courage.

Top, right.
A sad witness to the chaos of the night advance during the first phase of Totalize, this Canadian Sherman has fallen into a bomb crater near Cintheaux. It was recovered to be repaired later because on 9 August, the priority was to carry on moving southwards.
(H. Aikman, NAC PA-113707)

An armoured column belonging to the reconnaissance regiment of a Canadian infantry division (the Maple Leaf is visible on the left wing of the first vehicle) goes past the wreck of a Sturmgeschütz III Ausf.G. In the lead is a Humber Mk IV Armoured Car followed by a Humber Mk III Light Reconnaissance Car.
(H. Aikman, NAC PA-169068)

Totalize gets bogged down

During these unfortunate events, the second phase of Operation Totalize went ahead. Halfpenny's force, formed around the Grenadier Guards and the Lake Superior Rgt., faced very strong enemy resistance in front of Bretteville-le-Rabet.

Above.
Infantrymen from the Fusiliers Mont Royal patrolling in the ruins of May-sur-Orne on 9 August, searching for snipers lying in wait. The village has suffered terribly in the fighting; the church tower has almost been completely destroyed, clearly by artillery fire. The road has however already been cleared by the Royal Canadian Engineers.
(K. Bell, NAC PA-132419)

At 13.00, the Grenadier Guards had to withdraw and go to the rescue of Worthington's force and the infantry had to be strengthened by C Squadron of the South Alberta Rgt and the Argyll and Sutherland Highlanders, to finish clearing out the village. The Foot Guards and a company of the Algonquin Rgt., also sent to Hill 140, were blocked to the south of Langannerie by German Grenadiers supported by anti-tank guns and a Tiger lying in ambush.

An attempt to move round them on the right failed with heavy losses. The group retired onto a defensive position. Gradually realising that it was Worthington's force which was on Hill 140, the Canadians tried again to go to its rescue. The Grenadier Guards advanced south-eastwards but were stopped in the middle of a field between Bretteville and Estrées by very accurate Panzer and anti-tank gun fire: within a few minutes 26 Shermans were hit and the others ordered to withdraw.

Still spurred on by Simonds, the 4th Can. Arm. Div launched other units into the battle in order to reach its 9 August objectives. At about 15.00 the Argyll and Sutherland Highlanders accompanied by C Squadron of the South Alberta Rgt and the Lincoln and Welland Rgt supported by A Squadron from the same armoured regiment, attacked respectively Langannerie and Vieille Langannerie - Grainville. After fierce hand-to-hand fighting, these villages

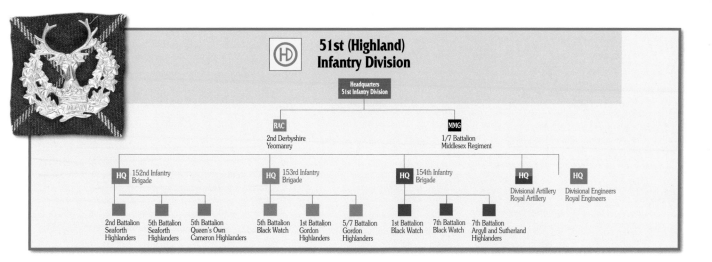

51st (Highland) Infantry Division

Headquarters 51st Infantry Division

RAC — 2nd Derbyshire Yeomanry

MMG — 1/7 Battalion Middlesex Regiment

HQ 152nd Infantry Brigade
- 2nd Battalion Seaforth Highlanders
- 5th Battalion Seaforth Highlanders
- 5th Battalion Queen's Own Cameron Highlanders

HQ 153rd Infantry Brigade
- 5th Battalion Black Watch
- 1st Battalion Gordon Highlanders
- 5/7 Battalion Gordon Highlanders

HQ 154th Infantry Brigade
- 1st Battalion Black Watch
- 7th Battalion Black Watch
- 7th Battalion Argyll and Sutherland Highlanders

HQ Divisional Artillery Royal Artillery

HQ Divisional Engineers Royal Engineers

---

were captured with the intervention of Typhoons. The infantry had already started digging itself in for the night when Simonds ordered a night attack. At 20.30 the Lincoln and Welland advanced towards Hill 180 to the south-east near Fontaine-le-Pin. Under fire from German machine guns, most of the troops reached their objective by nightfall and set up their positions but a company went astray and was encircled for a moment. The Argyll and Sutherland Highlanders set off at 23.30 to get hold of Hill 195 which Worthington's force had missed. From earlier reconnaissance missions it seemed that the Germans were only defending the western part of these heights. Using a

track not covered by the enemy, the Canadians marched in silence and without hindrance onto Hill 195 at about 5.00 and the position was taken almost without any fighting. They dug in rapidly, receiving some anti-tank gun reinforcements shortly afterwards in anticipation of a possible German counterattack. Kitching sent also the Foot Guards as reinforcements and for a moment even thought of launching them beyond to continue the breakthrough, but fire from the Nebelwerfers and anti-tanks guns bombarding Hill 195 at dawn was too vigorous and he decided against it. The SS-PzGrRgt.26's 3rd Battalion attacked several times using radio-controlled Goliath tanks but they

Below.
Near May-sur-Orne, a group of soldiers from the Fusiliers Mont-Royal examine a shattered Panther Ausf. A. which can only be from 12.SS-PzDiv., the only division to have this type of tank during operation Totalize. The turret has been blown off its seat by an internal explosion..
(K. Bell, NAC PA-1692 93)

45

were all driven off with the assistance of artillery, aircraft and armour. Aerial reconnaissance revealed the presence of twenty or so 88-mm cannon in the area and it became clear that an armoured attack by the Canadians was not going to be on the agenda!

THE POLES ADVANCE BUT SUFFER

Although blocked the day before, the Poles were not inactive on the 9th: towards midday, with the Cromwells from the 10th Chasseurs à Cheval leading, they set off to the south towards the N158 in the direction of St-Sylvain and Soignolles. Part of KG Wadmüller was reinforced by the escort companies from the 12.SS-PzDiv. and the I.SS-Panzerkorps together with the first elements of the 85.ID which was moving up; together they managed to hold onto their positions with the Hitlerjugend anti-tank guns destroying several tanks and armoured vehicles. The 1st Polish Armoured Division set off slightly south-eastwards and ended up overwhelming the first German positions. The 1st Infantry Battalion captured St-Sylvain during the evening but although almost entirely surrounded, Soignolles still held out. Meanwhile other elements of the 1st Polish Arm. Div. continued their thrust towards Estrées-la-Campagne. They came across some Canadian tanks which had escaped from Hill 140 and then tried to go to the rescue of Worthington's force during the afternoon but the German fire was too heavy and they could only gather in the survivors. Despite the fact that the second phase of *Totalize* was slowing down, Simonds still hoped that progress was possible and he reissued his attack orders for 10 August. In order to give the armoured divisions "a breather", he committed the 3rd Can. Inf. Div. and the 2nd Can. Arm. Brig. once again. The 8th Can. Inf. Brig. had to go through Quesnay Wood and could only start after 20.00. It was driven back brutally when it reached the edge of the wood (which was hardly surprising given that Meyer's Panzers had assembled there...). The Queen's Own Rifles of Canada and the North Shore Rgt. battled all night to hold onto their positions but had to withdraw at dawn with heavy casualties; above all they had been shot at by "friendly" artillery. Although the operation continued during the following days - mainly for the infantry to finish clearing out the German positions bypassed by the armoured columns - this last failure put an end to operation *Totalize*.

Right.
The soldiers in the 89.ID, just like those in the 85.ID, which arrived later in the month of August, were not among the best-equipped elite troops: this NCO has to make do with a heavy cloth combat uniform with reed-coloured chevrons but no particular camouflage pattern. On the other hand he is well-equipped with an MP40 and his trench spade has been slipped through his belt so as to be handy. The infantrymen on both sides very often dug into the Norman soil for shelter.
(Reconstruction.
© Militaria Magazine.)

Opposite page.
Armed with a captured MP40, a British soldier is rummaging through the ruins of the Chateau de Garcelles-Secqueville, which the Germans used as barracks; it belonged to the Comte de St-Quentin, apparently the senator of Calvados. Going by his helmet, the man belongs to an armoured unit, but the sign visible on his head gear does not correspond to any known Flash, and the caption of the period indicates that he belongs to the RAF... What is one to believe?
(IWM B8903)

A new offensive

The day after the end of Totalize, on 11 August 1944, Montgomery drew up a new directive (M518) which ordered the 1st Canadian Army and the 2nd British Army to move "quickly" against Falaise and to join up with the Americans.

THEY WERE HEADING TOWARDS ARGENTAN (they had in fact already gone past the town before the new operation was launched). Two armies were engaged because the "little encirclement" now had to be completed, according to Eisenhower's wishes - even if Montgomery's thoughts were increasingly turned towards the "big encirclement" which would enable even more German troops to be captured. Crerar and his staff started immediately organising the 2nd Canadian Corps' attack. Initially

called "Tallulah" (in honour of Tallulah Bankhead?), the operation was then called "Tractable". Simonds started work on this plan on 12 August in all haste and fixed the latest day for the start of the offensive as 14 August, leaving everybody with even less preparation time than for Totalize. As a result the Tractable plan of attack was nothing more than a slightly modified version of the previous plan: a shorter aerial bombardment would precede an attack by armoured columns followed by partly armoured

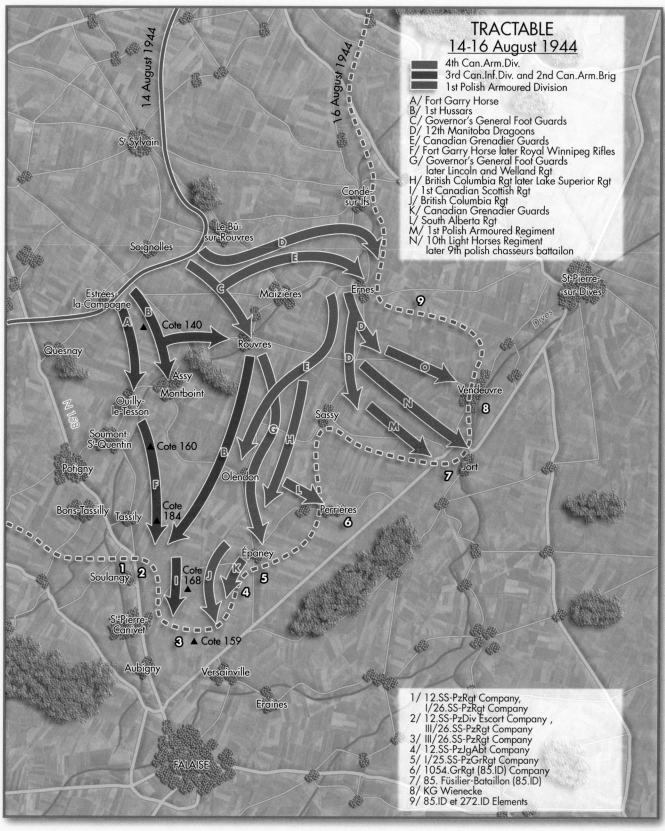

TRACTABLE
14-16 August 1944

4th Can.Arm.Div.
3rd Can.Inf.Div. and 2nd Can.Arm.Brig
1st Polish Armoured Division

A/ Fort Garry Horse
B/ 1st Hussars
C/ Governor's General Foot Guards
D/ 12th Manitoba Dragoons
E/ Canadian Grenadier Guards
F/ Fort Garry Horse later Royal Winnipeg Rifles
G/ Governor's General Foot Guards
   later Lincoln and Welland Rgt
H/ British Columbia Rgt later Lake Superior Rgt
I/ 1st Canadian Scottish Rgt
J/ British Columbia Rgt
K/ Canadian Grenadier Guards
L/ South Alberta Rgt
M/ 1st Polish Armoured Regiment
N/ 10th Light Horses Regiment
   later 9th polish chasseurs battailon

1/ 12.SS-PzRgt Company,
   I/26.SS-PzRgt Company
2/ 12.SS-PzDiv Escort Company ,
   III/26.SS-PzRgt Company
3/ III/26.SS-PzRgt Company
4/ 12.SS-PzJgAbt Company
5/ I/25.SS-PzGrRgt Company
6/ 1054.GrRgt (85.ID) Company
7/ 85. Füsilier-Bataillon (85.ID)
8/ KG Wienecke
9/ 85.ID et 272.ID Elements

14 August 1944
16 August 1944

St-Sylvain
Le Bû-sur-Rouvres
Soignolles
Condé-sur-Ifs
St-Pierre-sur-Dives
Estrées-la-Campagne
Quesnay
Maizières
Ernes
Dives
Cote 140
Rouvres
Ouilly-le-Tesson
Assy Montboint
Vendeuvre
Soumont-St-Quentin
Cote 160
Sassy
Potigny
Olendon
Perrières
Jort
Bons-Tassilly
Tassily
Cote 184
Épaney
Soulangy
Cote 168
Cote 159
St-Pierre-Canivet
Aubigny
Versainville
Eraines
FALAISE

N 158

infantry; the troops would however be moving in daylight but under the cover of a smoke screen.

At the briefing on 13 August, Simonds designated the objective- still the same one: Falaise, even if it was a now question of taking the heights which dominate the town. Indeed, in the original plan, capturing the town was to have been left to the 2nd British Army coming from the west. Simonds made it quite clear to his subordinates that the units would have to be pushed to the limit of their endurance and that he would not accept any excuses or any untimely pauses particularly during the night. His comments on the way operation *Totalize* was carried out were very critical of the soldiers and in

particular their officers, some of whom he would like to have got rid of but had not had the time. As with the earlier operation this one was carried out in two phases across a very narrow 2 miles front to the east of the N158 deliberately avoiding Quesnay Wood, the hub of German resistance.

CANADIAN STRENGTH

Lining up a total of about 480 tanks, 1 500 vehicles and 12 000 men in the assault troops, the 3rd Can. Inf. Div. and the 2nd Can. Arm. Brig. to the west, and the 4th Can. Arm. Div. to the east, were to head south or south-east from a departure line between Cauvicourt – St-Sylvain and the Estrées-Soignolles

Right.
In a heavily damaged farm near Rocquancourt, some soldiers from the South Saskatchewan Rgt. (2nd Can. Inf. Div.) relax after the fighting. After suffering heavy losses during Totalize, the division was only used for cover purposes during Tractable which did not prevent it from again suffering heavy casualties, particularly among the infantrymen of the Fusiliers Mont Royal and the South Saskatchewan Rgt.
(K. Bell, NAC PA-129136)

Below.
A column of Canadian vehicles going past Rocquancourt church and through the village on 11 August. A jeep and a light lorry no doubt towing a Bofors 40-mm canon are visible. According to the AoS sign on the jeep mudguard, this belongs to the second regiment of an infantry division.
(K. Bell, NAC PA-190014)

51

road. Each divisionary group was composed of three brigade-sized units. That of the 3rd Can. Inf. Div. was to be led by the tanks from the Fort Garry Horse to the right and the 1st Hussars to the left followed respectively by the motorised Stormont, Dundas and Glengarry Highlanders and by the Highland Light infantry (9th Can. Inf. Brig.), then by the North Nova Scotia Highlanders with the support of the armoured cars of the 17th Duke of York's Royal Canadian Hussars and finally by the 7th Can. Inf. Brig. For the 4th Can. Arm. Div. group, the 4th Can. Arm. Brig. was to lead the way (Governor General's Foot Guards on the right and the Canadian Grenadier Guards on the left) with the British Columbia Rgt. hastily re-formed in the rear and accompanied by the Lake Superior Rgt. They were to be followed by the 8th Can. Inf. Brig.: Régiment de la Chaudière on the right and the Queen's Own Rifles on the left, both motorised, and the North Shore Rgt on foot, to the rear, the 10th Can. Inf. Brig. bringing up the rear with the South Alberta Rgt. On the far left, the 51st Highland Division would cover their flank up to Bû-sur-Rouvres.

The armoured brigades would lead through 3 miles of German lines to set up the bridgeheads on the Laison. The two infantry brigades aboard the lorries and armour would follow in order to hold all the Laison between Montboint and Maizières and form a solid base for the second phase. A Squadron of Crocodile tanks from the 141st RAC was even attached so it could take part in clearing up the Laison valley. During *Totalize* too many enemy positions had been bypassed and left in enemy hands by the leading elements, delaying the following units' progress. The two other infantry brigades on foot would then pass through these positions and, following the tanks closely, advance 5 miles southwards up to the heights overlooking Falaise, about 1 to 3 miles from the town, at Epaney, Olendon and Perrières. As for the 1st Polish Arm. Div., it was assigned the secondary attack eastwards to capture Trun. Strong air support was requested again and the preliminary bombardment was to be carried out by the medium bombers of the 2nd Tactical Air force guided by the red artillery smoke flares on the defences of Montboint, Rouvres and Maizières.

Left.
The Canadians used the Wasp (Carrier flame-thrower) for the first time in combat during operation Tractable, but they also used the British "Lifebuoy" portable flame-thrower for clearing out villages after the armoured columns had passed through. This very effective model of flame-thrower however was not very popular with the troops because it was vulnerable and sensitive to gusts of wind: it was almost as dangerous for the user as for the target.
(Reconstruction. © Militaria Magazine. Coll. Ph. Guérin.)

Right.
Lance Corporal Bill Baggott rests on his motorbike, probably a Norton, before the beginning of the new offensive. Going by his belt and his ammunition pouch which have been painted white, he is a Military Policeman belonging to the Canadian Provost Corps as shown by the AoS 79 sign visible on the mudguard.
(M. Dean, NAC PA-161885)

Below.
Cintheaux, located on the N154 between Caen and Falaise, became an important crossroads for organising and deploying the forces used during operation Tractable. This Canadian half-track towing a trailer is going down one of the village streets devastated by the earlier fighting.
(Tank Museum 2985/B6)

Above.
On 10 August, the Canadian photographer-reporter, Ken Bell, took this shot in the quarry to the south of le Haut-Mesnil, littered with destroyed or abandoned German materiel. In the foreground, the front axle of an 88 mm FlaK 18, and behind this several lorries, including doubtless an Opel Blitz and perhaps a Krupp or six-wheeled Henschel.
(K. Bell, NAC PA-169295)

Typhoons and Spitfires could also be called in as often as needed. At 14.00 the British and Canadian bombers would attack 6 well defined targets: from west to east, Quesnay Wood, Aisy, Bons-Tassilly, Fontaine-le-Pin, Soumont-Saint-Quentin and the woods on Hill 206. As with *Totalize*, about 700 divisional artillery and 2nd Canadian Corps cannon would be held available for the initial barrage and for later support.

A WEAKENED BUT DOGGED ENEMY

The I.SS-Panzerkorps was still the Canadians' main adversary and had to defend Falaise at all costs because the town was the only way out for the encircled forces, now more than ever. The 89.ID had been trounced during *Totalize*, and could only hold a small part of the front to the west of the N158; to the east of the same road the much tried Hitlerjugend was relieved by the 85.ID under Generalleutnant Chill. This infantry division which had just come up in reinforcement was similar to the 89.ID: it was formed in February 1944 using disbanded units and new recruits; it had been stationed up until then in the north of France and had already taken part in the end of *Totalize*. As for the 12.SS-PzDiv., it lost 414 men during *Totalize* and on 12 August, part of its forces - the SS-PzGrRgt.26 HQ, a part of KG Waldmüller, two artillery batteries - had been withdrawn to re-form near the Seine. It could now only line up 35 tanks (including 17 Panzer IVs) and 2500 men around KG Krause, together with two

Right.
One of the Panzer IVs captured in August 1944 by the Anglo-Canadians is a well-known tank easily identifiable by the clumsily drawn numbers on the turret. It had already been photographed in Flanders at the beginning of 1944 and was from the 9th company of the II.PzAbt of the 12.SS-PzDiv. The tank commander was Oberscharführer Terdenge.
(Tank Museum 2364/A4)

The two Waffen-SS Tiger battalions present in Normandy were engaged to counter operation tractable, but they were already very much weaker and suffered heavy losses during the fighting. Here a Canadian soldier is examining the wreck of an end-of-production Tiger of the sSS-PzAbt.101's 2nd Company.
(Tank Museum 2397/A3)

companies of Jagdpanzers, the 1st Battalion of SS-PzGrRgt.25 and the 2nd and 3rd from SS-PzGrRgt.26, the remaining artillery and three Werfer batteries. The 88 mm cannon from its Flak regiment were fortunately still present, as were a reconnaissance group and the divisional escort company. It could also count on the 17 Tigers from sSS-PzAbt 101 and 102. The 271. and 272.IDs were still holding the flanks of the I.SS-Panzerkorps, respectively to the west and east.

The weak German defence supported itself on two lines about 2 miles apart. The infantry divisions constituted a rather light screen with a second, deeper line; it was not continuous but made up of support points, backed up by the Hitlerjugend with several 88s as anti-tank guns and dug in to the south along the valley of the Laison. Hill 159 in particular was well defended because it overlooked the Falaise – St-Pierre-sur-Dives road. Other 88s were positioned further back and the corps could bring to bear about 50 pieces in all. The divisional artilleries and the Nebelwerfers were further back, but there was no reserve behind them – the nearest German forces after them had their backs to them and were fighting the Americans on the other side of the salient barely 11 miles further south. The Germans did not sit there just waiting: they launched several localised counter-attacks from the 10th onwards but without any great success. Before *Tractable* set out, a reconnaissance en force was carried out by the 2nd Can. Inf. Div. on 12 August from Bretteville-sur-Laize towards the south. With the support of two AGRAs and two regiments of the 2nd Can. Arm. Brig., the division

progressed well before being intercepted at Cingal by four Tigers from the 2nd Company of the sSS-PzAbt 102. Four Shermans were lost for the price of one Tiger. The Royal Regiment of Canada took Moulines in the evening, 3 miles to the northeast of Potigny. On the following day, the Calgary Highlanders Rgt managed to form a bridgehead on the Laison at Clair-Tison, but the Regiment de Maisonneuve which took over the advance was repulsed with heavy casualties by the 271.ID supported by some Tigers. The 3rd battalion of the SS-PzGrRgt. 26 and its half-tracks had to remain on the spot to contain the bridgehead which was threatening the fragile flank of the German front.

It was now that an officer of the 14th Canadian Hussars got lost in his Humber Scout Car with his driver and crossed the enemy lines. He was shot and killed while trying to get away and the Germans found that he was carrying a copy of instructions received by the 2nd Can. Inf. Div. concerning *Tractable* together with a general plan of the attack. This unforgivable (and yet relatively frequent) mistake, which the Canadian officer paid for with his life, enabled the I.SS-Panzerkorps to redeploy its defences. Naturally there was not enough time to bring up reinforcements - which were almost inexistent anyway - but 88-mm guns and anti-tank guns were hastily brought up onto the hilltops overlooking the valley of the Laison. The result was a much higher casualty rate among the Canadian armoured regiments and in particular, the effect of surprise was completely lost: in spite of their weak forces, the Germans were ready and waiting to meet the Allied assault.

Tractable: the western flank

On 14 August, at 11.37 very precisely, the 25-pounders in the 2nd Canadian Corps opened up with red smoke flares to guide the medium bombers of the 2nd Tactical Air Force onto their targets at Montboint, Rouvres and Maizières.

MITCHELLS AND BOSTONS bombed their targets at 14.45 and ten minutes later a massive artillery barrage opened up along the 2 miles wide front between Rouvres and Montboint crushing the German defence under a deluge of explosive shells and smoke bombs which covered the assault forces. All efforts to concentrate the density of the screen were useless and visibility on the ground varied from 200 yards to only three! At the beginning of the barrage, the first armoured columns progressing along an eight-vehicle wide "front", got under way and reached an average speed of 12 mph up to the start line. At 12.00 when the armour started its southward charge, the second wave comprising 13 Canadian regiments or battalions (including one on foot) got going in turn to reach the departure line.

To the west the Fort Garry Horse and 1st Hussars tanks rushed on towards the Laison at Montboint, against resistance which had been diminished by the effect of both the preparatory air and artillery bombardment, and the fact that certain German units had withdrawn in anticipation of the attack. A little further on, Panzers and anti-tank guns fired

Above.
Two Churchill AVREs from the 79th Arm. Div. get ready to support the Canadian attack on 14 August. One of the tanks is carrying a fascine which was used to cross the Laison. The AoS 1233 sign visible on the other tank identifies the 5th Assault Rgt which was attached to the 2nd Can. Inf. Div. during Tractable. Note the bulldozer track and blade in the foreground.
(D. Grant, NAC PA-116523)

Above.
The ground crew of this Mitchell III, "Grumpy", belonging to n°98 Squadron RAF, are adding the symbol for the plane's 102nd mission (a record) on 14 August 1944 on the Dunfold airfield in Surrey. No doubt this plane has just taken part in the preliminary bombardment for Tractable.
(IWM CH13734)

into the confused mass of armour which was rolling along under a dense cloud of dust. Even without seeing a thing, they managed to destroy or damage twenty or so Shermans but this did not slow the Canadians down; they either completely overwhelmed the barrage-stunned defenders who started surrendering in large numbers, or merely went round the resistance points leaving them to the tender mercies of the following infantry. Sergeant Léo Gariepy of the 1st Hussars had to stop his Sherman in the lee of a few buildings to mend the trigger of his canon. A German officer came up to meet him and handed over the 280 men he commanded, all "volunteers" – Tartars, Mongols and Volkdeutsche who had been waiting for transport which would have enabled them to fall back...

During the first hour of the offensive confusion reigned because it was impossible to keep up the speed planned for the attack; but the German defence was incapable of stopping the attackers. The communication and navigation problems were almost just as enormous as during *Totalize*; the columns broke up rapidly and the sun, barely filtering through the dust and the smoke on occasions, became the only usable landmark... As a result the group behind the 1st Hussars found itself in front of the leading tanks and the armoured cars of the Royal Canadian Hussars overtook the vanguard of the Fort Garry Horse. The first columns of prisoners which were directed to the rear did not help to make the traffic any less congested.

LITTLE RIVER, GREAT EFFECT

The advance continued nonetheless and the Royal Canadian Hussars reached the Laison at 12.30 shortly before the 1st Hussars. This river

58

was only seven feet across and two feet deep but it turned out to be more of an obstacle than anticipated and had been neglected during the all-too short preparation before the battle. Indeed the banks of the Laison were steep and the river bed in particular was very muddy. Tanks trying to ford it got stuck immediately. Fortunately some fascine-equipped AVREs had been planned for this contingency but they were in the second wave so the tanks had to wait... At 12.55 Major Gordon, commanding

Above.
The armoured groups which followed the tanks during Tractable comprised miscellaneous elements capable of facing up to any contingency. Behind an Achilles M10 Tank destroyer armed with a 17-pounder, there is a Crocodile flame thrower, Carriers, Stuarts and Churchill AVREs.
(D. Grant, NAC PA-116525)

On 14 August, the 9th Can. Inf. Brig. (3rd Can. Inf. Div.) advanced aboard armoured vehicles from Bretteville-le-Rabet southwards and the regimental reconnaissance armoured cars of the division covered the flanks and scouted out in front. Here a Humber Mk III Light Reconnaissance Car is followed by a Humber Mk IV and a Carrier.
(D. Grant, NAC PA-171698)

B Squadron of the 1st Hussars, decided not to waste any more time. He followed the river course from Assy north-eastwards to find a passable ford, or even use the bridge at Rouvres.

But the banks were often wooded or too steep, or German gunfire was too heavy so they were unable to attempt a crossing, all the more so as there was nothing to show that the bottom of the river was not very muddy, either!

The 17 Shermans still operational reached the bridge at Rouvres towards 13.30 but the engineers already there confirmed that the structure had suffered too much damage to take the weight of vehicles. One tank tried to cross the river next to the bridge and got well and truly stuck. Gordon had to carry on into the village itself under enemy light arms fire. The reply from the Shermans' 75 mm guns and Brownings quickly silenced the Germans but this initial defence suggested that progress was going to get more complicated. Without finding a solution, Gordon returned to the bridge... to find that the Royal Canadian Engineers had filled in the damaged road surface with fascines. A first Sherman crossed over the bridge very gently. It held, so the other tanks followed slowly. The Squadron regrouped and was then able to drive south-westwards. The other two 1st Hussar Squadrons, after suffering heavy losses,

33rd Armoured Brigade (B)

From June 13th till August 15th, 1944

172
Brigade Headquarters

173
1st Northamptonshire Yeomanry

174
144th RAC

175
148th RAC

The Carriers in the 3rd Can. Inf. Div. towing anti-tank 6-pounders rush across fields southwards, following the tanks from the 2nd Can. Arm. Brig. The smoke screen has already lifted, but the cloud of dust raised by the Bren gun carriers is impressive.
(Tank Museum 2054/B2)

Above.
A Canadian half-track (on the original shot the Maple Leaf is just visible on the left wing) moves along the Falaise road. On its right wing an illegible tactical sign underlined in white indicates that the vehicle is attached to an army, therefore the 1st Canadian Army. According to the raised canvas top and the long aerial, this could be an armoured command vehicle.
(Tank Museum 2985/C5)

were able to cross to the east of Rouvres but had to re-form into a single squadron before being able to attack again. In fact it was the 7th Reconnaissance Rgt. armoured cars which were the first to cross the Laison over a small "forgotten" bridge but they had had to withdraw because of accurate German anti-tank gunfire.

Meanwhile the Fort Garry Horse also tried to cross the Laison at 13.15 to the west of Montboint, but ran into the same problems as the 1st Hussars. One squadron tried to approach the two neighbouring road bridges which were defended in strength by enemy grenadiers. The tanks without any infantry to accompany them had to withdraw under threat from the Panzerfausts. The regiment split up to go up and down along the river banks in search of a crossing point. To the east a little bridge near Logis Château enabled two squadrons to cross over and to head off towards Hill 184. The 2nd Echelon of the western group composed of the 9th Can. Inf. Brig. and the Royal Canadian Hussars followed the tanks. The Stormont Highlanders headed

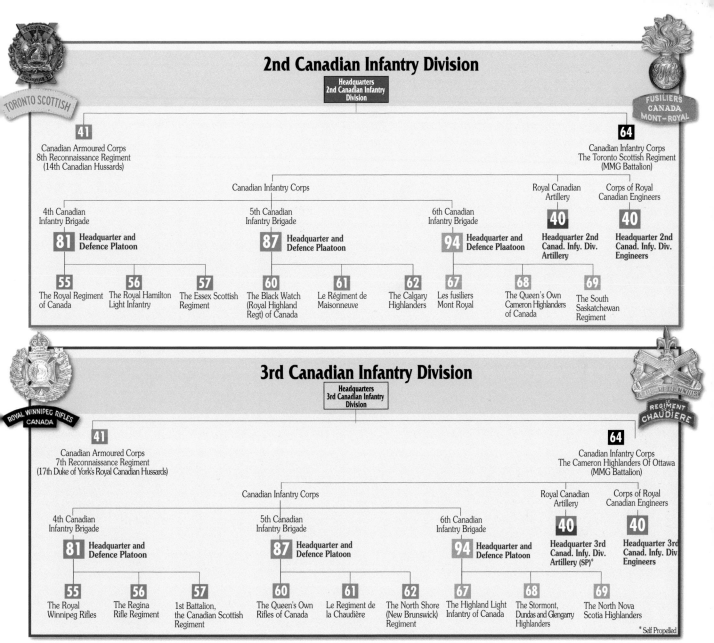

2nd Canadian Infantry Division

Headquarters 2nd Canadian Infantry Division

41 Canadian Armoured Corps
8th Reconnaissance Regiment
(14th Canadian Hussars)

64 Canadian Infantry Corps
The Toronto Scottish Regiment
(MMG Battalion)

Canadian Infantry Corps

4th Canadian Infantry Brigade — **81** Headquarter and Defence Platoon

5th Canadian Infantry Brigade — **87** Headquarter and Defence Plaatoon

6th Canadian Infantry Brigade — **94** Headquarter and Defence Plaatoon

Royal Canadian Artillery — **40** Headquarter 2nd Canad. Infy. Div. Artillery

Corps of Royal Canadian Engineers — **40** Headquarter 2nd Canad. Infy. Div. Engineers

55 The Royal Regiment of Canada

56 The Royal Hamilton Light Infantry

57 The Essex Scottish Regiment

60 The Black Watch (Royal Highland Regt) of Canada

61 Le Régiment de Maisonneuve

62 The Calgary Highlanders

67 Les fusiliers Mont Royal

68 The Queen's Own Cameron Highlanders of Canada

69 The South Saskatchewan Regiment

TORONTO SCOTTISH

FUSILIERS CANADA MONT-ROYAL

3rd Canadian Infantry Division

Headquarters 3rd Canadian Infantry Division

41 Canadian Armoured Corps
7th Reconnaissance Regiment
(17th Duke of York's Royal Canadian Hussards)

64 Canadian Infantry Corps
The Cameron Highlanders Of Ottawa
(MMG Battalion)

Canadian Infantry Corps

4th Canadian Infantry Brigade — **81** Headquarter and Defence Platoon

5th Canadian Infantry Brigade — **87** Headquarter and Defence Platoon

6th Canadian Infantry Brigade — **94** Headquarter and Defence Platoon

Royal Canadian Artillery — **40** Headquarter 3rd Canad. Infy. Div. Artillery (SP)*

Corps of Royal Canadian Engineers — **40** Headquarter 3rd Canad. Infy. Div. Engineers

55 The Royal Winnipeg Rifles

56 The Regina Rifle Regiment

57 1st Battalion, the Canadian Scottish Regiment

60 The Queen's Own Rifles of Canada

61 Le Regiment de la Chaudière

62 The North Shore (New Brunswick) Regiment

67 The Highland Light Infantry of Canada

68 The Stormont, Dundas and Glengarry Highlanders

69 The North Nova Scotia Highlanders

ROYAL WINNIPEG RIFLES CANADA

REGIMENT DE LA CHAUDIERE

* Self Propelled

for Assy and passed by Hill 140 and the wrecks of the British Columbia Rgt.'s tanks, an unhappy reminder of *Totalize*. The Highland Light Infantry, on the left, got scattered in the clouds of smoke, one company following the Stormont Highlanders, the other two wandering off eastwards where they crossed the 4th Can. Arm. Div.'s line of advance and continued for another 3 miles to Ernes!

The Stormont Highlanders progressed well and the infantry climbed down from their armour at 12.55 in the woods along the Laison.

Even though they were guarding the flank on the right, the 2nd Can. Inf. Div. had not remained inactive and in the morning, its 6th Inf. Brig. set

up its bridgeheads on the Laison then headed for Fontaine-le-Pin. The armour and the artillery could not follow since the only bridge available was blocked by two destroyed Shermans. A ford was found and the Sherbrooke Fusiliers were able to cross at around 7.00 to reinforce their defensive positions under cover of the morning mist. The fighting was fierce and German resistance was so strong that not all the objectives could be reached, particularly by the Fusiliers Mont-Royal, reduced to only two companies before the operation was launched. Moreover these units had also been hit by mistake in the heavy bomber air raid (see below) and the South Saskatchewan Rgt thus lost 65 men.

Tractable: the eastern flank

The first echelon of the 4th Can. Arm. Div. group set off at 12.00 towards the Laison between Rouvres and Maizières. Followed by the British Columbia Rgt. which had just been re-formed, the Governor General's Foot Guards and the Canadian Grenadier Guards led the columns.

THESE UNITS soon got mixed up in the confusion of smoke and clouds (some tanks even crossed the Laison three miles further east!); enemy resistance was scattered but tenacious, well supported by anti-tank guns and artillery. The ground markers had disappeared and the columns broke up rapidly and since the tanks following relied on those leading, the chaos could only increase. The officers in their Scout Cars went to and fro among the armour trying to obtain a semblance of order. In spite of everything, the road between Estrées and Maizières was reached towards 12.20. The infantrymen in the 1st echelon, Queen's Own Rifles and the Regiment de la Chaudière leading, followed by the North Shore Rgt, travelled very joyfully in 200 trucks: their shouts and singing could be heard through the clouds of smoke

and dust which were still just as dense (the distribution of an extra ration of rum was no doubt responsible for this enthusiasm ...)

Towards 13.00, the crews of the 4th Can. Arm. Div. discovered how much of an obstacle the river was. However, within three hours, thanks both to the reinforced fascine bridge at Rouvres and to several fords set up by the AVREs of the 80th Assault Squadron, and even a small bridge further east, all the armoured units managed to get across and were able to assault Hills 168 and 159 at 16.30. The British Columbia Rgt and the Lake Superior Rgt. had even made their own crossing using rubble. Meanwhile, behind the tanks, the 2nd echelon had also advanced towards the Laison which the motorised units reached at around 13.30. In the indescribable chaos, the infantrymen had to get down from their armoured vehicles and cross on foot. As for the three battalions

of the 10th Can. Inf. Brig. in their trucks who brought up the rear, they were only able to get started at 15.10. The artillery and the mortars had still not reached their firing positions from which they could support the troops and the only support they had was from those tanks present. However, the charge towards the Laison had been relatively successful overall, even if crossing the river had considerably delayed the advance. As on the western flank, the Engineers carried out sterling work clearing minefields or at least clearly signposting them, thereby reducing losses.

TRAGIC MISTAKE

But tragic events changed the course of *Tractable*. Between 14.00 and 15.30, 417 Lancasters and 352 Halifaxes dropped 3723 tonnes of bombs on the six targets as planned, to the east of the N158. Unfortunately once again, aiming errors

Above.
Operation Tractable was an opportunity for the Canadians (more exactly the 3rd Can. Inf. Div.) to use the Wasp flame thrower on a Universal Carrier for the first time. This impressive demonstration by the Queen's Own Rifles of Canada showing this little machine's power took place on 29 July 1944 near Vaucelles.
(D. Grant, NAC PA-130187)

Above.

Air support by Typhoons from the 2nd Tactical Air Force was available during the whole of Tractable from improvised airfields set up in Normandy on request from the ground troops. This Typhoon of n°82 Squadron RAF has been photographed on Base B6 at Coulombs, to the east of Bayeux.
(IWM CL890)

caused heavy casualties in the ranks of the Allied second wave. 77 bombers (including ironically, some belonging to the RCAF's 65th Group) dropped their bombs by mistake on their own troops causing between 100 and 150 killed and 250 to 300 wounded according to the sources. Lieutenant Belfield, an RAF pilot seconded to the 3rd Can. Inf. Div. as artillery observer, tried to prevent this massacre by taking off in his Auster to fly just below the bombers, firing his Verey pistol to stop them continuing, to no avail. This was all the more tragic because the initial drop itself was aggravated by the complete lack of communication between the aircraft and the troops on the ground. The latter, as soon as the bombs started falling among them used the yellow panels, smoke flares and rockets which normally indicated the Allied lines. But on that particular day, yellow was the colour the RAF had chosen to designate the targets for its bombers! Apparently Bomber Command was not

aware of the 2nd Canadian Corps' colour code...

Air Vice-Marshall Coningham of the 2nd Tactical Air force who had come to observe, was caught under the hail of bombs and was in the right place to judge whether or not the bombing was accurate... Lieutenant-Colonel Wotherspoon, commanding the South Alberta Rgt, who was being bombed for the second time by "friends", was on the point of ordering his anti-aircraft guns to open up but was prevented just in time from doing so by the regimental almoner, Captain Silcox. The 16th Battery of the 12th Field Rgt lost all its guns and all its transport. The Royal Regiment of Canada, resting near the Haut-Mesnil quarry was also severely hit and lost 26 vehicles and a lot of equipment but fortunately human losses were very light. This mistake compromised the future progress of *Tractable*, causing senseless losses, chaos and delay at a moment when the time factor was of the utmost importance once the element of surprise had been lost.

Above.
The 1st Polish Armoured Division moves on through the village of Quesnay which it has just liberated. According to the AoS sign beside the divisional insignia, the Carrier belongs to the Motor Battalion of the 10th Armoured Brigade, the 10th Dragoons (the division was formed up and equipped on British lines).
(Tank Museum 1424/E6)

Right.
The caption of the time says that this photograph shows German positions being pounded on 14 August. Unfortunately, it was the Allied lines which the RAF was bombing by mistake, most probably the quarry at le Haut-Mesnil, as witness the 15 cwt CWP truck in the centre and the excavator visible in the background on the right.
(K. Bell, NAC PA-132825)

The Poles took up the offensive again confidently on 15 August despite the difficult experience of their baptism of fire during Totalize. This Carrier usually armed with a Vickers machine gun belongs to the Machine Gun and Mortar Battalion of the 3rd Brigade of the Chasseurs, according to the AoS 64 sign, barely visible on the right mudguard.
(Tank Museum 1423/A4)

4th Canadian Armoured Division

Headquarters
4th Canadian
Armoured Division

45
Canadian Armoured Corps
29th Armoured Reconnaissance Reg.
(The South Alberta Regiment)

64
Canadian Infantry Corps
10th Independant Machine
Gun Company
(The New Brunswick Rangers)

Canadian Armoured Corps
4th Canadian Armoured
Brigade

50
Headquarter

Canadian Infantry Corps
10th Canadian Infantry
Brigade

60
Headquarter
and Defence Platoon

Royal Canadian
Artillery

40
Headquarter 4th
Canadian Ard. Div. Artillery

Corps of Royal
Canadian Engineers

51
21st Armoured Regiment
(The Governor General's
Foot Guards)

52
22nd Armoured Regiment
(The Canadian Grenadier
Guards)

61
The Lincoln
and Welland
Regiment

62
The Algonquin
Regiment

63
The Argyll
and Sutherland
Highlanders
of Canada

74
15th Field Regiment

76
23rd Field Regiment
(Self Propelled)

53
28th Armoured Regiment
(The British Columbia
Regiment)

54
The Lake Superior
Regiment
(Motor, Infantry Corps)

77
5th Anti-Tank
Regiment

73
8th Light-Anti
Aircraft Regiment

N.B.
RANGERS
CANADA

LINCOLN & WELLAND
REGT.

The afternoon of 14 August

At I.SS-Panzerkorps HQ everybody had understood that with the breakthrough the Laison no longer represented an obstacle for the Allies. With the losses accumulated over the previous days, the Germans could no longer continue suffering such high casualties and an urgent request for permission to retreat was therefore sent to the 5.Panzer-Armee.

BUT THIS WAS TURNED DOWN and they were ordered to hold the line at Soulangy. The situation moreover was even more critical to the west: the 271.ID's positions had been overwhelmed and the divisional HQ sent a final message to say it was being overrun by 30 tanks...a small group of the 12.SS-PzRgt had to be rushed there to remedy the situation since the British were now only 3 miles from Falaise.

Once the Laison had been crossed and the bridgeheads established, the Canadians had to resume the attack towards the heights to the south. But there was a problem at one of the bridgeheads. On the 3rd Can. Inf. Div.'s front, A Company from the Stormont Highlanders advanced towards Ouilly-le-Tesson and St-Quentin capturing a lot of prisoners, while B and C Companies cleared out the German defence at Assy with difficulty. B Company pushed on south-westwards; suddenly it was stopped in its tracks by the crossfire from four machine guns in GrRgt 1053 of the 85.ID. A Tiger lying in ambush 900 yards away prevented anybody going round by the right and other machine guns did likewise on the left. At 17.00, in order to avoid further losses, the attackers called in a section of three Wasp flame

Above.
Canadian infantrymen greeting the crew of a Humber Mk IV Armoured Car from the reconnaissance regiment of one of their infantry divisions (cf AoS 41 sign on the right wing). The Canadians showed a lot of drive during Tractable, just as if they sensed that the Normandy campaign was nearing its end.
(Tank Museum 1015/A1)

Photographed in July 1944, the crew of Tiger N°231 belonging to Obersturmführer Loritz, belonging to the 2nd Company of the schwere SS-Panzer Abteilung 102 is examining the engine through the large rear hatch. The Waffen-SS's 2nd Battalion of heavy tanks still had 31 tanks left of which one third was still operational and joined the front to the north of Falaise on 9 August.
(ECPAD)

throwers on a Carrier chassis – used for the first time in combat by the Canadians. They deployed over roughly a 110 yards front and advanced slowly, throwing out incandescent jets neutralising the three machine gun nests as well as the grenadiers' trenches. The fourth machine gun servers fled and the infantry was able to get hold of the much-coveted bridges in fifteen minutes.

Meanwhile, the 2nd Can. Arm. Brig. group was ready to resume the offensive again from Assy towards Hill 184, but at 16.30 only. Near Montboint the Fort Garry Horse set off on its second charge of the day towards Hill 160 which it reached at 17.15. The Royal Winnipeg Rifles who were following them on foot pushed on towards the approaches to the road between Tassilly and Soulangy and stopped there at nightfall. In this sector the Hitlerjugend escort company supported by a company of Panzers defended its positions fiercely and the Canadians were forced to dig in for the night after advancing more than 2 miles beyond the Laison.

Slightly further on, B Squadron from the 1st Hussars tried twice to push on from Rouvres southwards but to no avail. Losses were heavy and it was a group of only nine Shermans that managed, on the third attempt, to break through the anti-tank screen, crush the enemy guns under their tracks

and rush to Hill 111. The other two squadrons in the regiment had the same objective but they started further east and ran into less resistance. The 1st Hussars ended up by stopping to the west of Olendon, slightly further back from the Fort Garry Horse. They had to attack at night however with the 1st Canadian Scottish Inf. Rgt to get hold of Hill 171. Tank losses were high, but progress was satisfactory. The 7th Can. Inf. Brig. closed the day when the Winnipeg Rifles relieved the tanks in the woods between Olendon and Tassilly, littered with enemy bodies and equipment. The Regina Rifles set off at 18.00 to join Polish elements at Estrées in order to keep the nearby Quesnay Wood under fire.

THE GUARDS STRUGGLE

To the east the 4th Can. Arm. Brig. had difficulty reorganising after the death of its CO, Brigadier Booth. His replacement, Lieutenant-Colonel Scott of the Foot Guards was very quickly designated but divisional HQ, whose communications had suffered during the "friendly" bombing, did not know that this officer was in fact wounded and was only able to join his post at nightfall. Without a brigadier for six hours, the three armoured regiments continued their advance in a rather disorderly manner, wandering off to the east and having difficulty reaching their objectives. The Foot Guards and the

Above.
On 14 August, the same Tiger 231 belonging to Loritz was destroyed by the Canadians near Ussy during Operation tractable; there were no survivors. The discoloured right flank, where the Zimmerit has also completely disappeared, shows that this part of the Panzer probably caught fire and burned.
(DR)

Right.
The 1st Armoured Division in Normandy was entirely equipped with both clothing and weapons by Britain. This Polish NCO has therefore donned a British battledress but has kept his Polish insignia, in particular the characteristic collar patches and his marks of rank on the beret. This way of wearing the beret, sloping rearwards with the insignia in the centre was characteristic of the Poles. The British wore the beret inclined on the right with the insignia above the left eye.
(Reconstruction.
© Militaria Magazine.
Coll. L. Taveau.)

Grenadier Guards resumed their attack at around 16.30 in the direction of Olendon, still followed by the British Columbia Rgt. This regiment had almost been decimated during *Totalize* and had been re-formed as well as possible, but the replacement tanks had arrived so late that there had been no time to paint the tactical markings on them. The squadron commanders were incapable of recognising their own troops!...

The Foot Guards set up a departure base in the woods 1 mile north of the village and were soon joined by the Grenadier Guards and the Régiment de la Chaudière. These three units held onto the position to enable the Argyll and Sutherland Highlanders and the Lincoln and Welland Rgt, with the support of a squadron of the South Alberta Rgt each, to launch their assault on Olendon at 17.15. While the British Columbia Rgt attacked on the flank, the main group advanced frontally, got hold of the village in 30 minutes against weak resistance and set itself up rapidly in defence.

Reconnaissance showed that Perrières, 1 miles to the south-east had been abandoned, as Gr. Rgt. 1054 had withdrawn. The Argyll and Sutherland Highlanders took the village and neighbouring Hill 115 during the night. Passing to the east of Olendon, the Algonquians managed to reach the north of Epaney with the Lake Superior Rgt. which had routed a column to the north of Perrières and taken 250 prisoners. At the end of the afternoon, the left flank of the offensive was secured and when the exhausted North Shore Rgt. infantrymen who had crossed the Laison came into sight of Sassy it was the Carrier platoon who charged and took the village against ferocious resistance from the 85.ID Fusilier Battalion which was quickly eliminated. The 12th Manitoba Dragoons armoured cars which were patrolling between Sassy and Ernes signalled that the enemy was withdrawing. They made contact with the 51st Highland Division who had also suffered from the bombing mistakes but had got hold of Bû-sur-Rouvres in the evening.

At midnight on 14 August, the results of the first phase of *Tractable* were encouraging. A 6 miles x 5 miles breach between Quesnay Wood and Ifs-sur-Laison, had been made with the loss of only 370 men (not counting those caused by "friendly" aircraft!) and almost 1 000 prisoners had been taken. Simonds was rightly satisfied with this result and was not expecting anything less the following day... On the Canadian side, the night was given over to bringing in the stragglers, bandaging wounds and resupplying. But the Germans also used the night to spread out their meagre available forces, nearly all of them from the Hitlerjugend:as well as they could. In spite of support from Wünsche's Panzers, a lot of men from the 85.ID had surrendered. The Jagdpanzers made up several defensive points to the north/north-east of Falaise, the 12.SS-PzRgt. supported what was left of the 85.ID which kept in touch with the 272.ID to the east, and KG Krause was reinforced by two Tigers, taking

This Panther Ausf.A belonging to the 12.SS-PzDiv. was photographed on 14 August at the entrance to Soumont-Saint-Quentin, near Potigny. On this date, Kampfgruppe Wünsche only had ten or so Panthers still operational, just...
(ECPAD)

up position on the northern edge of the town. The Hitlerjugend artillery together with the Werfer Rgt. 83 crossed over onto the south bank of the Ante where they discovered an abandoned ammunition depot which enabled them at last to support the German defence properly – which had not been the case for a long time in Normandy!

Unfortunately the Flak battalion, as well as all other Luftwaffe forces, were withdrawn in spite of the 5.Panzer-Armee's protests and an enormous anti-tank potential was thereby lost.

Right.
Another Panther Ausf.A from the same unit in Soumont-St-Quentin on the same day. This is a Befehlspanzer, a command tank, which can be recognised by the two antennae, of which one is a parasol aerial. Unlike the tank above, this Panzer has not been camouflaged with leaves at all, an exception during the Normandy campaign.
(ECPAD)

Second wind?

When the attack resumed on 15 August, the German defence had got itself together again and the 2nd Canadian Corps advanced desperately slowly. Towards midday Hill 184 was captured by the Fort Garry Horse and the Winnipeg Rifles, and to the far west, the 2nd Can. Inf. Div. was put in to the line and managed to progress from Clair-Tison south-eastwards.

Above.
This Sherman, probably a command tank, could not have been more aptly named: "Warszawa", to express the long-awaited revenge the Poles were going to exact from the Germans, in Normandy to start with, then across the whole of Europe into Germany.
(Tank Museum 2709/A6)

ELSEWHERE, the fanatical resistance the enemy put up prevented any significant progress being made. The 7th Can. Inf. Brig. was ordered to take Falaise but the Winnipeg Rifles failed to take Soulangy after being driven off by KG Krause with heavy losses in spite of support from the 7th Recce Rgt. On this very narrow front which prevented more than three battalions being deployed at a time, the 1st Canadian Scottish Rgt, accompanied by a few tanks and tank destroyers, headed towards Hill 168,

2 miles away to the north of Falaise. From 12.00 onwards three companies, supported by 1st Hussars tanks, moved along the Soulangy-Epaney road. Facing them was the 3rd Battalion of the SS-PzGrRgt. 26 lying in ambush with nine Panzers and sweeping the open terrain with its fire. At 13.00, without support from the artillery which had not yet joined them, the Canadians launched their assault and immediately ran into deadly fire from four machine guns. Three Tigers kept the Shermans at bay and

the infantry, which included a lot of recently-arrived young recruits, dug in too hastily. Officers and NCOs had go to and fro under fire to persuade their troops to advance to what was to all intents and purposes a protective hedge... which turned out to be defended by the grenadiers concealed just behind it!

After an exhausting, but successful, hand to hand fight the infantrymen had still to advance over more open ground and to clear out slowly and meticulously all the enemy machine gun posts, under constant mortar fire and under threat from two Tigers which were finally driven off by several PIAT rounds, but not without first destroying ten or so Shermans. Three other Panzers were dislodged in the same manner before the infantry was able to reach Hill 168 at 17.15, reinforced by the last company. German resistance was still fanatically desperate with Panzers wandering around on all sides firing confusedly at friend and foe alike. The SS refused to surrender, one of them shot himself in the mouth rather than give up. But the Canadians ended up taking the hill without the help of the Regina Rifles who had not moved up for lack of armoured support and after losing 127 men (one company was reduced to 46 men only).

To the east, the 1st Polish Armoured Division finally entered the fray with renewed passion, because the 15th was "Soldier's Day" in Poland. The previous day the division had occupied Quesnay Wood and taken Potigny and Fontaine-le-Pin where the soldiers funnily enough freed some Polish miners. Corporal Stefan Barylak of the 24th Lancers, a Polish immigrant who had left France at the time of the occupation to join his compatriots in London, even had the emotion-charged possibility of going past his own house in Gouvix! For the time being the Poles headed towards Jort to set up a bridgehead over the Dives there and then carried on to Courcy and Trun. The Cromwells from the 10th Chasseurs à Cheval Regiment led the charge. One of their tanks was destroyed by a Panzerfaust at Vendeuvre where the bridge over the Dives had been blown up. They were also attacked by their own 1st Armoured Regiment who thought they were the enemy! The 9th Battalion of Polish Chasseurs took over leading the column, but the river could only be crossed during the night. With the 4th Can. Arm. Div., the Foot Guards reached Hill 168 while the Algonquians, Lincoln and Lake Superior Rgts. captured Epaney in spite of the desperate defence by an SS-PzGrRgt. 25 company reinforced by a handful of Jagdpanzers. The Germans held the south-western edge of the village, but the Canadians succeeded in infiltrating and digging themselves in, protected by the tanks at the bottom of Hill 159. Two companies left in the woods to the west of the village had to be pulled back however after several hours of very fierce fighting had weakened them.

Epaney was bypassed to the west by the Grenadier Guards and the British Columbia Rgt who advanced cautiously southwards and towards Hill 159, barely a couple of miles from Falaise, but without either infantry or artillery support and under heavy fire from enemy anti-tank guns, mortars, a company of Panzers from SS-PzRgr. 12 and field artillery, the two regiments had to fall back suffering heavy losses. The Grenadier Guards only had 33 tanks left instead of about sixty. Simonds was furious when he learnt of this failure, all the more so because he had been told earlier by mistake that the objective had been taken! Moreover, instead of pushing on southwards, the 4th Can. Arm. Div., already stuck on most of its lines of attack, had to go to the rescue of the 3rd Can. Inf. Div. whose situation was getting more and more complicated.

Below.
On 16 August the Canadians were still leading groups of prisoners taken during Tractable back to the rear. A column of twenty or so prisoners is being escorted by two Canadian infantrymen, near le Haut Mesnil. Operations Totalize and Tractable marked the "beginning of the end" for the German defence to the south of Caen.
(D. Grant, NAC PA-135954)

On the evening of 15 August, the offensive had not only run out of breath, it had almost stopped altogether. Although the German lines had been breached and resistance reduced to sniper or artillery fire, the offensive hardly resumed during the night. The 10th Can. Inf. Brig. defending Epaney and Perrières, was liberally bombarded by enemy artillery and mortar fire and the 9th Can. Inf. Brig. got ready to relieve it during the evening. A gathering of 150 enemy armoured vehicles along with lots of troops was spotted in the woods to the south of Perrières. This estimate was no doubt exaggerated, given the state of the German forces by that date. Whatever... 32 Typhoons intervened against this group and the threat was considered as averted at the end of the day. Against the 271.ID's weakening defences, the 2nd Can. Inf. Div. progressed well towards Falaise during the night but slowly. The 6th Can. Inf. Brig. advanced towards Ussy and Villers-Canivet, and the two other infantry brigades, after relieving the Poles on Hill 206, marched on Falaise from the north and west. The night was dark and it was raining; communications were bad and advancing at night was fraught with difficulties. On the morning of the 16th, the three battalions of the Royal Regiment of Canada (4th Can. Inf. Brig.) got lost for a moment because their maps had got soaked by the rain and were illegible but they finally managed to reach the heights overlooking Falaise.

Simonds got ready to launch his attack when Crerar informed him in the afternoon of the 15th that, although Falaise was still an objective to be taken and by the 1st Canadian Army at present, the main objective had now moved more to the east. Its two armoured divisions had to get hold of Trun as quickly as possible and join up with the US 3rd Army and close the Falaise Gap once and for all, since the German retreat was clearly speeding up. Crerar learnt from Montgomery that elements of the 5.Panzer-Armee were counter-attacking near Argentan, but this same army had ordered its units at 21.00 the previous evening to start evacuating the Falaise Gap and this without Feldmarschall von Kluge's consent. Operation *Tractable* was officially terminated on the 16th in the morning. In the end, the breakthrough was 7 miles deep and 7 miles across. This was appreciable but Falaise was still in German hands, so at most this was only a half-victory.

Right.
The state these German prisoners, captured on 8 August between Tilly-la-Campagne and Hubert-Folie are in shows the shock of the heavy bombardment and the Totalize night attack. Worn out, covered in dust and ragged, some of these soldiers seem to be happy to have escaped hell.
(H. Aikman, NAC PA-131369)

Arguably a failure

Operation Totalize has too often been decried as a complete failure, yet another one, for Montgomery in his effort to break out to Falaise. One has to get away from all the big statements pronounced before the attack promising a final, once and for all, breakthrough, and stick to the facts.

THE FIRST PHASE OF *TOTALIZE* has to be taken as a success, considering German equipment losses and casualties just as much as Allied territorial gains, particularly in the light of previous offensives in this sector of the Normandy front. On the other hand, the second phase very quickly got bogged down and caused excessive human and material losses for relatively mediocre results. The British and Canadian armoured attacks in Normandy have often been criticised for being

The initial success of *Totalize* was mainly due to the originality of the plan of attack, to the strength of the means committed, to the relative effectiveness of the bombardments, the night marches, the element of surprise, etc. For example, using Priests/Kangaroos was a real brainwave, as witness the lower attrition rate for the motorised infantry compared with the columns on foot. During the advance, Canadian infantrymen in the armoured columns only lost 7 killed and 56 wounded compared with 68 and 192 for their marching comrades respectively (even though the latter were twice the number initially, the difference is still significant). The Canadian and British assault is still praiseworthy in spite of the confusion reigning everywhere. On the other hand, the advantages which made a night attack successful no longer existed during the second phase. The element of surprise was lost, the air raids were counter-productive since they hit the "friendly" lines, the Germans had time to reinforce, and although taking place in full daylight, navigation mistakes were very frequent and more serious, viz. the destruction of Worthington's force on Hill 140. Moreover, the two armoured divisions attacked along too narrow a front, one normally intended for a single division.

Above.
Title and Cap badge of 29th Armoured Reconnaissance Regiment (South Alberta Regiment).

DEFINITE PROGRESS

Nonetheless the front did progress to the south of Caen and the breach they had made was 10 miles deep and 8 miles wide (at its widest) and indeed threatened the German front with total collapse. The breakthrough greatly disorganised the German troops: the II.SS-Panzer-Korps had to place itself under the command of the 7.Panzer-Armee because there was no longer any contact with the 5.Panzer-Armee. Because of the Anglo-Canadian offensives, there was no longer any coherent enemy front to the north of the gap, where there were only isolated resistance points. And yet Falaise was still in the hands of the enemy, some 8 miles from the Canadian forward positions. It was therefore vital to launch a new large-scale offensive, operation *Tractable*, to reach this most important objective. And the results of *Tractable* were even more modest than for *Totalize*, even if its first phase was relatively successful. Using two untried armoured divisions to lead the assault was not necessarily the right choice because they did not have the necessary experience to take advantage of all the opportunities. The 4th Can. Arm. Div. was sometimes too cautious and although the 1st Polish Arm. Div. did not lack boldness, its combat inexperience led it to make costly mistakes. It is also true that Montgomery was starting to lose interest in Falaise and was looking much more to the Seine; no doubt as a result, all

Previous page.
After the fighting, this Sherman called "Fitzroy II", which had tried to ford the Laison at Rouvres is still bogged down in the riverbed. The Class 40 Bailey Bridge set up after it failed to wade across is clearly visible on the left. Members of the Royal Canadian Engineers are studying a way of getting it out of its unfortunate posture.
(D. Grant, NAC PA-131270)

over-cautious but it has to be remembered that the Sherman crews were fighting in tanks whose armour and armament were very often inferior to that of their adversaries. They were vulnerable to all enemy tank cannon and anti-tank guns; moreover their 75-mm gun was incapable of penetrating the armour of the most powerful Panzers (Panthers and Tigers) at normal combat ranges. In spite of all this and bearing in mind the sight of all those fire-blackened, battered perforated Shermans littering the battlefields, going in to attack an adroit and determined adversary across open country must surely demonstrate the courage of those crews, many of whom did not return unscathed from combat...

Mid-August 1944, dozens of Canadian tanks and armoured vehicles stretched out across the vast plain to the south of Caen; in spite of the relative failure, Totalize and Tractable did however bring the German forces very near to the brink, and although the Panzers were indeed a real threat for the Allies units, this was only occasionally and until the Falaise Gap was closed.
(IWM MH28256)

the necessary means were not made available to support the 2nd Canadian Corps and the combination of heavy losses and fatigue began to tell and reduce its effectiveness.

ADVANTAGE TO MONTY

For both operations, the lack of time meant that the complex plans of attack were not prepared well enough. The unwieldy chain of command and the lack of both flexibility and, with a few exceptions: individual initiative, were in fact features of the 21st Army Group. The planning was rigorous and precise but there was no scope for improvisation, which is particularly important and decisive in a battle of movement. In addition there was no accurate intelligence. For example, the High Command knew as little as the units about the weakness of

the German reserves for *Totalize* which made them excessively cautious and as a result they held back the impetus of the attack instead of letting it go. Likewise, if French civilians had been questioned before *Tractable*, they would have said that the Laison was a difficult river to cross. The halt made during *Totalize* to wait for the heavy air raid, and the overall halt to fighting at night gave the Germans too much time to get themselves together and being past masters in the art of defence and improvisation, they always had the opportunity to reorganise their feeble defences before the following assault. The point at which the German front could be destabilised was reached several times, but that little extra "nudge" which would have obtained victory quickly never came. With commendable concern for the lives of their men, Montgomery and his

generals put their faith in using mechanical and material strength to defeat a redoubtable foe who, unlike them, was prepared to sacrifice his men to secure the outcome of the battle. The tactical and fighting qualities of the German soldiers were superior at all levels of the military hierarchy and they mastered modern combat techniques better than the Anglo-Canadians. In this respect, the tactic of using a mass of armour supported by artillery and heavy bombers was much more like the Soviet "steam roller" than a cavalry charge! The results were often disappointing, as during operations *Totalize* and *Tractable*, but the objectives were frequently reached. Even though Victory did not always keep its appointments, more Allied soldiers than German ones saw the sun rise the day following the battle...

Previous page, bottom.
***The Hitlerjugend Division,
already sorely tried,
came out of the fighting
battered by Totalize
and Tractable and only
played a secondary role
after 15 August. This
15 cm Grille Ausf.M self-
propelled gun belonging
to the division whose
insignia is quite visible on
the left on the casemate
armour has probably
been abandoned because
it has run out of fuel.***
(Tank Museum 62/A2)

Bibliography

- **The Canadian Soldier,**
  Jean Bouchery, Histoire & Collections
- **The British Soldier, vols I and II,**
  Jean Bouchery, Histoire & Collections
- **British tanks in Normandy,**
  Ludovic Fortin, Histoire & Collections
- **A fine Night for Tanks,**
  Ken Tout, Sutton Publishing
- **Road to Falaise,**
  Stephen Hart – Battle Zone Normandy, Sutton Publishing
- **Steel Inferno, I SS Panzer Corps in Normandy,**
  Michael Reynolds, Spellmount Publishers
- **Hors-Série SteelMasters n°16** "Opération Totalize"
  Hors-Série SteelMasters n°19 "La poche de Falaise (1)",
  Histoire & Collections
- **D-Day Canadian Forces Operations 1-23 August 1944,**
  MLRS
- **The History of 79th Armoured Division,**
  Anonyme, 1945

- **The Royal Canadian Armoured Corps,**
  John Marteinson, Michael R. McNorgan, RCACA-RBS
- **Normandie 1944, l'été canadien,**
  Bill McAndrew, Donald E. Graves, Michael Whitby,
  Art Global
- **Bataille de Normandie, 11 juin-29 août 1944,**
  Ouvrage collectif, Heimdal
- **The Guns of Normandy,**
  George G. Blackburn, McClelland and Stewart
- **The black Devil's March,**
  Evan McGilvray, Helion & Company
- **Armor Battles of the Waffen-SS 1943-45,**
  Will Fey, J.J. Fedorowicz Publishing
- **Stalingrad en Normandie,**
  Eddy Florentin, Presses de la Cité
- **Tigers in Combat II,**
  Wolfgang Schneider, J.J. Fedorowicz Publishing
- **Fighting the Breakout,**
  Edited by David C. Isby, Greenhill Books

This book has been realised by Denis Gandilhon.
Conception, make-up and realisation by Gil Bourdeaux and Matthieu Pleissinger.

All rights reserved. No part of this publication can be transmitted or reproduced without the written consent of all the autors and the publisher.

ISBN: 978-2-35250-053-7

Publisher's number: 35250

© Histoire & Collections 2008

Histoire & Collections
SA au capital de 182 938,82 €

5, avenue de la République
F-75541 Paris Cédex 11

Tel: +33-1 40 21 18 20 / Fax: +33-1 47 00 51 11
www.histoireetcollections.fr

This book has been designed, typed, laid-out and processed by *Histoire & Collections* and *"le Studio Graphique A & C"* on fully integrated computer equipment.

Color separation: *Studio A&C*

Print by Elkar, Spain, EEC.
May 2008